CITY
TO
CITY

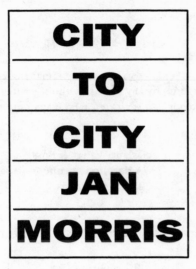

CITY
TO
CITY
JAN
MORRIS

MACFARLANE WALTER & ROSS

TORONTO

Macfarlane Walter & Ross
37A Hazelton Avenue
Toronto, Canada
M5R 2E3

CANADIAN CATALOGUING IN PUBLICATION DATA

Morris, Jan, 1926—
City to city
Most essays previously published in Saturday night.
ISBN 0-921912-10-2
1. Canada — Description and travel — 1951–1980.
2. Canada — Description and travel — 1981–
3. Canada — Social life and customs.
4. Cities and towns — Canada.   I. Title.
FC75.M67   1990   971.064   C90-094995-3
F1017.M67   1990

Printed and bound in the United States of America

For
RON GRAHAM
with affection and gratitude

*I owe my thanks
to the editors of* Saturday Night, *Toronto,
who first commissioned
most of these essays.*

CONTENTS

INTRODUCTION

MY VERY FIRST MEMORY
of Canada is everybody's first memory of Canada, whether actual or imaginary. In it I am standing in an open doorway of
a train at night — a steam train, whose smoke, generally in-
visible in the dark above us, now and then reveals itself in a
shower of sparks. The train moves noisily but inexorably, apparently rather slowly, rackety-rack, rackety-rack through the
night. Behind my back the tiered bunks of the sleeper car are
all shrouded in curtains, with dim lights glimmering in the
corridor down the middle. Outside millions upon millions
of trees stand black against the limitless snow, and in their
shadows my recollection vaguely shows me elks, and bears,
and beavers, and foxes — trappers too, paddling their canoes
down interminable rivers, and Indians, and priests, and swag-
gering half-castes in thonged leather jerkins.

Of course I did not really see those people and creatures in
the forest, but for the rest my memory is genuine. I was taking
part in a trans-Canada lecture tour in the winter of 1953, and
the one image of the venture that remains overwhelmingly in
my mind, nearly forty years later, is the vision of that dark
wooded immensity seen from the pounding rackety train.

It is an image the whole world has of Canada, as though the

place is buried somewhere in the universal collective uncon-
scious. The size of it, the emptiness, the challenges of ice and
wilderness, the sense of power that has always been particularly conjured up by railways — these are what most people
intuitively and immediately think of when they consider the
idea of Canada.

There is truth enough to the reaction — political and historical truth, as well as aesthetic truth. Over the years since
1953, though, I have come to feel that it is a misleading
truth. Canada is one country whose parts are greater than
the whole, and its colossal scale is becoming increasingly
irrelevant. The detail is what really counts now, and it is
far more interesting, if only because it has had to survive
against such overwhelming physical odds. There are times
and places in Canada when I think — we probably all think
— that one would have to be crazy to live there; yet it is not
craziness at all, but a somewhat mysterious and evidently
contagious instinct. On the map, and on the face of things,
Canada is one of the least magnetic places on earth, yet it
is one of those two or three countries where half humanity
would prefer to reside; not just in Toronto, Montreal, or Vancouver, either, but in places like — well, you know the sort
of place.

It was not always so. For years half the British emigrants
who went to Canada went there only in the hope of going
to the United States, and I remember even in the 1970s being told by a Turk that if you lived to a ripe old age in Canada
you died of boredom. For years I myself used to say that much
the best road in Toronto was the one that led to Manhattan.
Perhaps, however, there comes a time in the lives of nations

when a personality is finally formed, creating its own magnetism, generating its own energy, and that time has clearly
come in Canada.

This is ironic, for it has come at a juncture when, at least
to the outsider's eye, Canada seems only half-resolved to con-
tinue as a nation at all. On the one hand its anglophones and
francophones seem congenitally unable to share a common
nationhood amicably. On the other its citizens of all origins
sometimes appear to have lost heart in the old struggle to
maintain a national identity in the shadow of the United
States. More and more often I hear people saying that there
is really no important difference between ways of life north
and south of the border, that indeed Canadianness is more or
less the same as Americanness.

I fight these flaccid contentions vehemently. The more often I have visited this country, in the years since that night
prospect from the Canadian Pacific sleeper door, the more
clearly I have come to realize that Canada is unique. It is
pure nonsense to say that it might as well be part of the
U.S.A. — almost nowhere in Canada could I suppose for
a moment that I was on American soil. Not only is there
the utterly distinct French element, not only are the political and social systems quite different, but the whole temper of life in Canada, its manners, its looks, its values, I
think, are unmistakably Canadian. Few would deny that it
is less exciting than the United States, but Americans often
themselves concede that in many fundamental ways it is su-
perior.

Almost despite myself I have come to identify with this frequently perverse nation. Presumptuously I feel myself to be

on its side in its battle with destiny. I think it deserves better of itself — more recognition of its own virtues, more readiness to blow its own trumpet, a little less becoming diffidence, a bit more vulgar swagger. Sometimes Canada's modesty touches me, but sometimes it makes me feel like giving it a kick in the seat of its ample pants, to get its adrenalin going.

This collection of essays, then, records not just a change of perceptions, but a growing involvement. Since 1953 I have written about Canada many times, either as an element in British imperial history, or just as itself. I have come in many circumstances. Sometimes it was only a stopover at Gander, in the days when trans-Atlantic flights often had to refuel there, and I can still feel the sudden tang of the northern air that hit us before we laboured on our piston-engined way. More often I came to do a job of work. For historical purposes, for instance, I followed the fur traders into the wilderness, the gold-prospectors up to the Yukon, the Royal Navy to Esquimault. I did readings at a couple of literary festivals, and once or twice American magazine editors sent me trailing from coast to coast in search of generalizations.

I often thought that one day I might write a book about the country, but I could never devise a literary shape for it. I was still obsessed with the enormous unwieldy whole of Canada; like the old railway-builders, I felt that some grand uniting conception was necessary to make sense of such a prodigy. It was only when the Toronto magazine *Saturday Night* invited me to write a series of essays about Canada that I realized the binding element could lie not in the general but in the particular: not in metaphors like that of the passing forest from the train at night but in the examples of individual places, each investigated as a separate entity, without much reference to any of the others but amounting nevertheless to a foreigner's view of the nation as a whole.

So this is a book that ignores the size of Canada. There are, I hope, no statistics in it. Nowhere does it say that Canada is the biggest, the emptiest, the richest, the widest from coast to coast, the nearest to the Pole. There is not much more about the trees and the trains. It is specifically an urban view of the country, and does not pretend to be anything like comprehensive. I offer it simply as a somewhat random portrait, expressing no more than artistic responses of an impressionistic kind.

I fear those responses may irritate some of my readers as being testy, superficial, selective, impertinent, or, worst of all, patronizing. However, if there is incivility to the work, it is certainly unprovoked. I can remember experiencing hardly a word of rudeness, or an inhospitable gesture, during the writing of these pieces, and this has only confirmed me in my conviction that Canada, while it may not be the most thrilling of countries, has a genuine claim to be considered the best.

JAN MORRIS
Trefan Morys
1990

CHAPTER ONE

ST JOHN'S

A smack in the face with a dried cod

O*F ALL THE CITIES I HAVE written about, anywhere in the world, none has given me more enjoyment than St John's, Newfoundland, the most entertaining town in North America.*

It was as a historian of the British Empire that I first went there, thirty-odd years ago, Newfoundland having occupied a unique place in the imperial scheme of things, and St John's having remained until recent times an anachronistic curiosity among imperial towns. By the time I came to write this essay the Empire's effects had long faded, and they were

1

*different excitements that beguiled me, but I remembered
with particular affection an incident from my original visit,
in 1956, that said a lot about the continuing character of St
John's.*

*In the Newfoundland of those days it was necessary to
find a local guarantor before one could cash foreign money
orders. Knowing nobody in town, and discovering that the
public library had a copy of a book of mine about Venice, I
introduced myself to the librarian and asked her to endorse
a traveler's cheque. How could she confirm, she sensibly
demanded, that I was who I said I was? By a simple literary
test, said I; surely nobody else on earth could recite by heart
the last line of my Venetian book, which she had upon her
own shelves.*

*Solemnly she reached for the volume. Nervously I stood
at her desk while she turned to the final page, and ran her
eye down the paragraphs to the end of it. Well? she said. I
cleared my throat. The concluding words of my book were
not very stately.* "No wonder," *I mumbled them, feeling dis-*
tinctly disadvantaged, "no wonder George Eliot's husband
fell into the Grand Canal." *Without a flicker that librarian
of old St John's closed the book, returned it to the shelf and
authorized my money.*

T HWACK! DESPITE IT ALL,
the personality of St John's, Newfoundland, hits you like
a smack in the face with a dried cod, enthusiastically
administered by its citizenry.

2

The moment you arrive they take you up Signal Hill, high above the harbour, where winds howl, superannuated artillery lies morose in its emplacements, and far below the ships come and go through the rock gap of the Narrows. Within an hour or two they are feeding you seal-flipper pie, roast caribou, partridgeberries, or salt cod lubricated with pork fat. They introduce you to the mayor, John "Rags" Murphy. They show you the grave of the last Beothuk Indian and the carcass of the final Newfoundland wolf. They remind you that they, alone in continental North America, live three and a half hours behind Greenwich Mean Time.

They chill you with tales of the corpses lying in Deadman's Pond. They warm you up with Cabot Tower rum. They take you to the site of the city's first (hand-operated) traffic signal. They show you the house into which the prime minister of Newfoundland escaped from a lynch mob in 1932, and the field from which the aviators Harry G. Hawker and Kenneth Mackenzie-Grieve unfortunately failed to cross the Atlantic in 1919. They guide you down higgledy-piggledy streets of grey, green, yellow, and purple clapboard. They explain to you in detail the inequities of the 1948 Confederation referendums. They tell you repeatedly about their cousins in Boston, and involve you in spontaneous and often incomprehensible conversations on street corners.

Such is the nature of this city; windy, fishy, anecdotal, proud, weather-beaten, quirky, obliging, ornery, and fun.

I start with "despite it all" because St John's is undeniably a knocked-about sort of town. Economic slumps and political hammerings, tragedies at sea, sectarian bigotries, riots, fires, poverty, and unemployment — all have taken their toll, and make the little city feel a trifle punch-drunk.

The very look of it is bruised. The outskirts of St John's are much like the purlieus of many another North American city — malls, car dealers, airport, duplexes, a big modern university — but its downtown is bumpily unique. Set around the dramatically fjord-like harbour, overlooked by oil tanks and fort-crowned heights but dominated by the twin towers of the Catholic basilica, its chunky wooden streets clamber up and down the civic hills with a kind of throwaway picturesqueness, suggesting to me sometimes a primitive San Francisco, sometimes Bergen in Norway, occasionally China, and often an Ireland of long ago.

"Either it's the Fountain of Youth," said a dockyard worker when I asked him about a peculiarly bubbling sort of whirlpool in the harbour, "or it's the sewage outlet." St John's is nothing if not down-to-earth. The shambled slums I remember from twenty-five years ago have been miraculously abolished, but the best efforts of the conservationists have not deprived the town of its innate fishermen's fustian. The most enlightened restoration of its streets has not managed to make it self-conscious. The first dread fancy lampposts and ornamental bollards, the first whiff of novelty-shop sachets, the arrival on the waterfront of that most ludicrously incongruous architectural cliché, mirror-glass — even the presence of Peek-a-Boutique in the premises of the former Murray fishery depot — have so far failed to make St John's feel in the least chichi. It remains that rarity of the Age of Collectibles, an ancient seaport that seems more or less real.

I hear some expostulations, nevertheless. "Fishermen's fustian," indeed! For all their hospitality, I get the sensation that the inhabitants of St John's may prove prickly people to write about, and there is a prejudice I am told among some of the grander St John's persons (we can no longer, I suppose, call them St John'smen) against the city's association with the fish trade.

Yet even the loftiest burghers' wives could hardly claim that this is a very sophisticated place. It is like a family city, meshed with internecine plot, but still somewhat reluctantly united by blood, history, and common experience. It is the poorest of the Canadian capitals; it has little industry and few great monuments; its responses are those of a permanently beleaguered seaport on a North Atlantic island — which is to say, responses altogether its own.

Actually within the city limits of St John's there are pockets of the probably spurious Arcadianism that Newfoundland picture postcards so love to show. Small wooden houses speckle seabluffs, dogs lie insensate in the middle of steep lanes, and here and there one may still see the fish stretched out to dry, as they have been stretched for 400 years, on the wooden flakes of tradition. Almost within sight of Peek-a-Boutique I met a hunter going off to the hills in search of partridge, buckling his cartridge belt around him, hoisting his gun on his shoulder, just like a pioneer in an old print. And immediately outside the windows of one of the city's fancier restaurants ("Step Back in Tyme to Dine") one may contemplate over one's cods' tongues the whole rickety, stilted, bobbing, seabooted, genial muddle that is the classic image of maritime Newfoundland.

It really is a community of cousins, too. I happened to notice on a monument one day that the now defunct police force called the Newfoundland Rangers numbered, among its Guzzwells, Stucklesses, and Snelgroves, a disproportionate number of Noseworthys. So I looked up that clan in the St John's telephone book: 305 are listed, by my count, including Randy Noseworthy, Ethel Noseworthy, Dwayne Noseworthy, Franklin Noseworthy, Major H. Noseworthy, and Noseworthy, Keating, Howard and Kung, Accountants — their names constituting in themselves, I thought, a proper register of St John's social consciousness.

It happened that while I was in town St John's was celebrating its centenary as a municipality with what it called a Soiree — generally pronounced swarr-ee — and recalling a favourite old Newfoundland song:

There was birch rine, tar twine,
Cherry wine and turpentine,
Jowls and cavalances, ginger beer and tea,
Pig's feet, cat's meat, dumplings boiled in a sheet,
Dandelion and crackies' teeth at the
Kelligrews's Soiree. . . .

The festivities closed with a public party at the St John's Memorial Stadium that powerfully reinforced the family illusion, and suggested to me indeed an enormous country wedding — everyone someone else's in-law, everyone ready to talk, with no pretence and no pretension either. Noseworthys were numerous, I do not doubt, and Kelligrews were certainly there in force, though content no longer with ginger beer and tea.

Jigs and folk songs sounded from the stage, miscellaneous bigwigs sat stared-at in the middle like rich out-of-town relatives, and when people seemed slow to dance, jolly Mayor Murphy took the floor alone, offering free booze coupons to any who would join him — "You have to get them half-tight," he remarked to me as he handed out these inducements, jigging the while himself.

The pubs of St John's are mostly less than trendy. The downtown corner store flourishes. The St John's *Telegram* carries not merely death announcements but long and sometimes extremely gloomy poems to go with them, such as:

He's gone, oh gone for ever,
The one we loved the best.
Our days of joy are ended
As the sun sets in the west.

"Your mouths are so big they could fit in a zoo," a member of the city council told his colleagues in plenary session during my stay. "You're a sook," responded the deputy mayor.

I puzzled, as every stranger must, about the mingled origins of this pungent civic character, and the first strain I identified was undoubtedly the Irish. The simplicity of St John's is streaked, I came to sense, with a particularly Irish reproach, wit, and irony — sometimes I felt that Ireland itself was only just out of sight through that harbour entrance. The prickly pensioners and layabouts who hang around on Water Street, "The Oldest Continuously Occupied Street in North America," look pure Cork or Wexford. The instant response that one gets from nearly everyone is Ireland all over. And

7

the complex of buildings that surrounds the Basilica of St John the Baptist, episcopal, conventual, didactic, societal buildings, is a reminder that here Irish values and memories, however dominant the British colonial establishment of the place, proved always inextinguishable.

But that establishment too still flies its flags — literally, for at city hall they flaunt not only the ensigns of the city, the province, and the Confederation but actually the Union Jack too, for reasons defined for me as "purely sentimental." This was a self-governing British possession within my own lifetime, after all (no school stamp collection of my child-hood was complete without the 1¢ Caribou of our oldest colony), and within the city centre it is still easy enough to descry the old power structure of the Pax Britannica. The governor's mansion is recognizably the social fulcrum that it was in every British colony. The garrison church is spick-and-span. The Anglican cathedral is authentically unfinished, like all the best Anglican cathedrals of the Empire. The old colonial legislature is properly pillared and stately, and down the hill is the Supreme Court building, smelling of warm wood and depositions in triplicate, which once also housed the prime minister's office, responsible directly to the Crown in London.

Indeed, as a sign reminds us on the waterfront, The British Empire Began Here — when Sir Humphrey Gilbert establish-ed the first permanent settlement of New Founde Land in 1583. The city is appropriately rich in heroic memorials, commemorative plaques, royally planted trees or dukely laid foundation stones (though as a matter of fact, St John's be-ing St John's, the stone laid by the Duke of Connaught in

Bowring Park in 1914 turns out to be the thriftily recycled headstone of a dog's grave). Kipling himself worded the plaque at the site of Gilbert's landing, Field Marshal Earl Haig unveiled the Water Street war memorial. Nor are the imperial loyalties merely lapidary: one devoted monarchist drives around town with British flags stuck on her trunk and flying from her radio aerial, and another was not much pleased, I fear, when I suggested that in Britain itself royalism, like cigarette smoking, was primarily a lower-middle-class enthusiasm. . . .

"Not that the British," even these zealots are quite likely to say, "ever did much for Newfoundland." On the contrary, the general view seems to be that London behaved as negligently towards its oldest colony as Ottawa does to its youngest province. Most people I asked said that emotionally at least they would prefer to enjoy the independence signed away to Canada in 1949, but a good many told me that if they had the choice they would opt for union with the U.S.

This did not surprise me. In some ways St John's is very American. It does not feel to me in the least like Canada, being altogether too uninhibited, but I can conceive of it as a half-Irish, half—Empire Loyalist backwater of New England. A century ago the Newfoundlanders were all for free trade with the Americans, at least, and would have got it if the British government had not intervened; today half the people I met seemed to have American connections of some kind or another, mostly in Boston. When I suggested to one elderly lady that closer links with the United States might in the end mean more corruption, exploitation, and general degradation, she seemed quite affronted. "That's only the *fringe* of things down there," she said.

But I looked her in the face as she said this, and I rather think I detected in it, through the patina of the years, the bright eager features of a GI groupie of long ago. I know of nowhere in the world where the American soldiers of the Second World War are remembered with such affection, or where, perhaps as a result, the equivocal colossus of the south seems to be given the benefit of so many doubts. "I can assure you that at heart the Americans are very good people," my informant firmly added, and as we parted I swear I heard, as in historic echo, a giggle in the shadows of McMurdo's Lane, and a distant beat of "In the Mood."

These varied inheritances and associations save St John's from any suggestion of provincialism. History does it, one might say. The fateful gap of the Narrows is like a door upon a world far wider than Canada itself, while the city's particular kinds of expertise, to do with ships, and fish, and ice, and seals, and perilous navigations, make it a place beyond condescension. Memorial University of Newfoundland has a formidable reputation, the Marine Institute is world-famous, and ships of many nations and many kinds, perpetually coming and going through the harbour, give the town a cosmopolitan strength — rust-streaked fishing vessels from the deep Atlantic grounds, hulking coastguard ships, coastal freighters, ocean research vessels, container ships and warships and ships bringing salt for the winter roads — ships in such ceaseless progress that each morning of my stay, when I walked down to the waterfront before breakfast,

I found that some new craft had come out of the night like a messenger while I slept.

The historical continuity of St John's, too, allows it a status beyond its size. The Grand Banks, which brought the first Europeans to these parts, still figure inescapably in its affairs, and the matter of the 200-mile fishing limit profoundly affects not only the economy of the port but its very style. Gone, like enemy aliens from a land at war, are the Iberian fishermen who used to bring a Latin emollient of wine and lantern light to this northern waterfront, but the statue of Our Lady of Fatima in the basilica, presented by grateful Portuguese mariners in 1955, pointedly remembers still the long Romance connection.

Then the matter of St Pierre-Miquelon, St John's own foreign-relations issue, is really a last irritant from the Seven Years' War, which ended in this very city 227 years ago. Though the islands are familiar enough to St John's people (university students go there for French-language immersion courses), their presence somewhere over the southern horizon queerly haunted my thoughts in the city — so resolutely foreign still out there, so utterly separate, a department of France behaving, so close to Mayor Murphy's homely bailiwick, with such absolute damned Frenchness.

The world has been passing through St John's certainly for a longer time, and perhaps with a greater intensity, than through any other Canadian city — from the Basques, Dutch, French, and English of the early years to the GIs of the Second World War and the Russian and Japanese seamen who are familiars of the place today. All their influences have been absorbed, in one degree or another, into the city's persona. To take two oppositely alcoholic examples (for St John's loves its drink): the rum called Newfoundland Screech, born out of the eighteenth-century Caribbean saltfish trade, is bottled in St John's to this day, while Newman's Celebrated Port Wine, originally sent here to mature because the long sea voyage from Europe was said to have a beneficial effect upon it, is offered still under the antiseptic auspices of the Liquor Corporation.

Such range, for a city of 100,000 souls, longitude 52.43 W, latitude 47.34 N! No wonder St John's, though long reduced to the condition of a provincial capital, remains so defiantly itself. There is no false modesty here. "You're right, but it isn't true of St John's," a man told me when I remarked that the citizens of most Canadian cities wanted to talk about nothing but themselves — and he went on to rehearse in loving and elaborate detail all other superiorities of the civic character.

In fact the people of St John's are irresistible talkers about themselves, and their peculiar accent, which strikes me as a cross between Irish, Devonian, and Atlantic Seal, makes the flow of their infatuation all the more unguent. Since everyone seems to know nearly everyone else, throughout my stay I felt myself encompassed within a web of overlapping reminiscence, amusement, and complaint. Gossip flows lively in St John's; images of scandal, joke, and mischief passed before me like figures on a wide and gaudy screen. The moneyed dynasties of the town, the Ayres, the Jobs, the Harveys, the Outerbridges, were dissected for me in richest idiom whether living or extinct; politicians suffered the sharp sting of Newfoundland iconoclasm; as I was guided around

12

the streets one by one the pedigrees and peccadillos of their structures stood revealed. Here was the store which was all that was left of the Xs' fortunes, here the mansion where the wildly successful Ys resided. One of the less estimable of the lieutenant governors lived in this house, a whiz-kid entrepreneur had lately installed eight bathrooms in that, and down by the waterfront was the not very upmarket department store whose ownership had given Mayor Murphy his affectionate nickname.

All this makes life in the city feel remarkably *immediate*. There is no lag, it seems, between introduction and confidence. By my second day in town I was being given under-the-counter comments on the local judiciary by a well-known politician. By my third day I was being treated to the lowdown about some spectacular financial goings-on. Hardly had I been introduced to a member of one of St John's oldest families, who has one house in town and another on its out-skirts, in a kind of Newfoundland version of the transhumance system — hardly had I met this distinguished citizen and his wife before they were explaining why their cat is named after — well, I had better not say who it's named after, let alone why.

I was walking along a city street one day when a man sweep-ing leaves launched upon me without warning an obviously political statement in such advanced Newfoundlandese that I can only reproduce it impressionistically, so to speak, with the help of a glossary of the dialect. It sounded something like: "Sish yarkin trapse John Murphy, tacker snarbucklerawny yok John Crosbie, glutch aninst Suzanne Duff." He looked at me expectantly for a response, so I simultaneously shook my head and nodded, to be on the safe side.

1 Extend Arm (*says a notice at a pedestrian crossing outside city hall*)
2 Place Foot on Street
3 Wait Until Cars Stop
4 Thank Driver

It struck me as a quintessentially St John's announcement, with its blend of the amiable, the unexpected, and the tongue-in-cheek. If reading this essay makes you too feel rather as though you are being slapped in the face with a dried codfish, that is because I was beguiled by almost everything about the city and its inhabitants (almost, because I do wish they wouldn't smoke so much . . .). I dare say that if the long-promised oil bonanza ever happens the town will ruin itself with affluence, but I rather think not: it is too rooted in the satisfaction of being utterly unlike anywhere else.

The standard history of St John's is a monumental two-volume work by Paul O'Neill. One might expect such a labour of municipal devotion to be heavy going; in fact it is one of the most consistently entertaining history books I have ever read, full of excellent stories, gamy characters, and surprising historical allusions. Similarly, every corner of old St John's offers its own intriguing details. At 100 Water Street there is the sweetly old-school china shop that the Steele family has run for more than a century, while not far away the Neyle-Soper Hardware Store displays in its windows, like *objets d'art* in a museum, grandly Newfoundland things like paraffin lamps, hatchets, scythes, and mousetraps that catch four mice at a time. There is a shop that sells nothing costing more than three dollars, and a shop that sells Young Seal Carcass at forty-nine cents a pound, and Kim Le's Tailor Shop with tailoring visibly taking place inside. Above the old lovers' steps of McMurdo's Lane the starlings roost in their noisy thousands.

See that object on the rooftop there? That's the periscope of a German U-boat, mounted triumphantly above the Crow's Nest Club, which was a famous haven of the convoy captains in the Second World War. See those wagons beyond the dockyard? That's the rolling stock of the narrow-gauge Newfoundland Railway, forlornly immobilized here because the railroad no longer exists. Hear that bang? That's the gun on Signal Hill, fired each day at noon as it was in the days of the redcoats.

As for the concrete city hall, it is a very repository of the civic self-esteem. Such banners and plaques and portraits and statues and old municipal photographs! Such ship models and armorial bearings and fraternal messages from admirals, mayors, and societies of merchant venturers! When I remarked how proper it was that the mayor's own office should look directly down upon the historic waterfront, somebody said yes, and directly down upon his own store, too — such is the organic frankness of this close-hauled sceptic town.

I was conscious always all the same, as I wandered so enjoyably through the city, that life and history have never been easy here. Beneath the charm there lies a bitterness. St John's is full of disappointment, and is an exposed and isolated place in more senses than one. One afternoon, by

driving the few miles out to Cape Spear, I made myself for
a moment the easternmost person in North America, and was
chilled to think, as I stood there in the wind, that while at
my back there was nothing but the ocean, before me there
extended, almost as far as the imagination could conceive,
the awful immensity of Canadian rock, forest, prairie, and
mountain. St John's is the edge of everywhere, the end and
start of everything. The sign for Mile "O" of the Trans-Canada
Highway stands immediately outside city hall; it was on Signal
Hill that Marconi received the very first radio communication
from across the ocean. Hawker and Grieve failed indeed to
fly across the Atlantic from St John's, but Alcock and Brown
succeeded, and here one evening in 1927 people hearing the
drone of an aircraft ran outside to see Lindbergh's *Spirit of St
Louis* disappear into the twilight for Paris.

And to this day, though much of the activity of St John's
has moved inland, everything in this city looks down, if only
metaphorically, to the Narrows. Even the stolid Confederation
Building, erected with a becoming diffidence well back from
the bloody-minded seaport, peers cautiously from its distance
towards that dramatic fissure. I found myself bewitched by it:
repeatedly driving up to its headlands, or around the southern
shore to the lighthouse at the end, or waving goodbye to the
ships as they trod carefully between the buoys towards the
open sea — a distant slow wave of an arm, from wheelhouse
or forecastle, returning my farewell as seamen must have
responded down all the centuries of Atlantic navigation.

Once I was contemplating that hypnotic view from the bar
of the Hotel Newfoundland, which looks immediately out to
the Narrows and the Atlantic beyond. It was evening, and the

prospect was confused by the reflection, in the plate-glass windows, of the people, plants, and ever-shifting patterns of hotel life behind me. Beyond this insubstantial scene, though, I could see the stern outline of the cliffs, the floodlit Cabot Tower on Signal Hill, the white tossing of the ocean breakers, and the slowly moving masthead light of a ship sliding out to sea.

The hotel pianist was playing Chopin — and as he played, with the recondite inflections of Newfoundland conversation rising and falling around me, mingled with laughter and the clink of glasses, somehow the riding light of that ship, moving planet-like through the mirror images, brought home to me with a *frisson* the grand poignancy that lies beneath the vivacity of St John's. I thought it sad but exciting, there in the air-conditioned bar.

CHAPTER TWO

ST ANDREWS

A *call to prayer*

I OFTEN FEEL A TUG OF THE
*emotions in Canada, generally when I like something, or
for that matter dislike something, despite myself. All too
frequently it is because, cherishing as I do generally radical
if not actually anarchist views, I find myself unexpectedly
sharing attitudes nostalgic or even reactionary — in many
ways Canada is a profoundly conservative country. It has
never quite developed into love-hate — there is not much
to hate in this essentially benign state — but it does, I am
sure, sometimes create that inner tension of the emotions*

that in literary terms is liable to show itself in sneer, gush, or condescension.

I hope no such solecism shows itself in this essay about St Andrews, New Brunswick, because I grew very fond of the town and its inhabitants. Many of the things they stood for did indeed jar with my own sensibilities, and made me suspect that if I actually lived there I might become an insufferable civic maverick; but as it was, during my ten days in town the citizenry won me over, and left me unforeseeably sympathetic to all their postures and pretensions.

Almost all, anyway. And sometimes despite myself.

IF, ONE SUNDAY MORNING, you chanced to come by sea to St Andrews, New Brunswick, prudently noting the state of the twenty-eight-foot tide, navigating a trifle nervously, perhaps, through the shoals, islands, and fish weirs of Passamaquoddy Bay, and tying up at the municipal wharf close to the wooden hut that is the Men's Club in winter, the Tourist Bureau in the summer season — if you were to sail in at eleven o'clock on a Sunday morning you would be challenged by a formidable cacophony of bells.

There would be the bell of the venerable Greenock Kirk, which has a fine sculpted oak tree on its tower, and the bell of the United Church, which is prettily steepled, and lavish recorded peals would issue from All Saints' Anglican Church, whose rector is the Venerable Archdeacon J.F. Nantlais Jones, and to complete the ensemble a carillon would sound solemn but sickly, as carillons do, from the United Baptist Church, an exquisite little job in the style known around here as Carpenter Gothic. All at the same time every Sunday (only the Catholic bell rings earlier) they fling their music magisterially across the water, clanging, clashing, chiming, donging.

Talk about a call to prayer! If I were some fierce Iranian ayatollah, sailing thus into Canada, I think I might decide to unfold my tents elsewhere. As it is, being only an inoffensive Welsh agnostic, and arriving as it happens prosaically in a rented sub-compact from Edmundston, I myself interpreted the bells not as a defiance exactly but certainly as a declaration of intent. "We Have Spent 200 Years," says a St Andrews tourist slogan, "Preparing For Your Visit!" — but that should not be regarded, I distinctly sensed when the carillon ran down at last, as an invitation to take liberties.

There was little chance, either, of sneaking in unobserved. I came to St Andrews in the early summer, before its permanent population of some 16,000 had been doubled by seasonal visitors. An inquisitive stranger in the streets was hard to miss then, and evidently almost as hard to ignore — when I went out for a walk that Sunday afternoon the very first person I met, an affable small boy, asked me if I would care to cuddle his gerbil Checkers, which was at that moment emerging from the neck of his shirt. St Andrews has virtually no suburbs, standing as it does all by itself at the end of a peninsula, and its heart consists of six parallel streets, perhaps a mile long, crossed by twelve others running down to the waterfront. You can

walk its perimeters in forty-five minutes, if not too delayed
by gerbil-fanciers, and I found that, after having read Mrs.
Grace Helen Mowat's history of the town, and mugged up a
bit on the Civic Trust's architectural pamphlets, and talked
to a few more people on sidewalks, I felt quite familiar with
the social structure of St Andrews.

Who was this, for instance, smiling at me so kindly from the
Wren House on Queen Street? Why, who but Miss Lelia Wren,
who lives with her sister Miss Frances in the house their
family has occupied for 150 years? Who is at the helm of that
white boat out there? Mr. Mered Hatt the scallop fisherman,
of course — everyone knows that. In no time at all I was
acquainted with Mr. Ian MacKay, who owns the Shiretown
Inn and much more of downtown St Andrews, and with Mrs.
Bobby Cockburn, whose late husband's pharmacy was one of
the town's prime power centres, and very soon the Venerable
Nantlais Jones was waving to me from his handsome Buick
Park Avenue limousine, which has CLERGY in ecclesiastical
lettering on its windshield.

There goes Town Councillor Hugh Akagi, descendant of
the Micmacs who frequented this peninsula long ago. Here
comes Mrs. Eleanor Mawson the archivist, homeward from
her labours in the former jail (where the last execution took
place in 1942). Outside the trim Town Hall stands Mr. Wade
Simmonds, who rings the municipal bell four times a day in
season, to the annoyance of nearby hotel guests, and walking
along Water Street I spot Maestro Lewis Dalvit, who comes
up from Mississippi every year to run the town's summer arts
festival. Hardly has one well-known householder introduced
me to her stately collection of teddy bears ("That's Boogy,

that's Oogy, that's Daddy Bear in the corner") before another is telling me how effective birth-control pills have proved in the propagation of her hibiscus plants.

It was like exploring a rambling old family home, the streets its corridors, the houses its rooms, the citizens its extremely gossipy owners and retainers. One morning I arranged to meet two of the town's many widows, to pick their brains about the civic character; and idly passing the time beforehand by wandering through the town cemetery (the only graveyard I know overlooked by a children's tree house, propped above the tombs), I found both those ladies' names already inscribed upon gravestones, below their departed husbands'.

Many of these people had recently been to a Party. I give it a capital P because it had been, I gathered, unquestionably the party of the year, thrown to celebrate the centennial of the Algonquin Hotel, the famous half-timbered hostelry that occupies a gentle hill above the town, and has for years dictated its social stance.

Oh, everyone told me, I really *should* have been at that Party! Lady NB was not there alas, but Lord A was, and the provincial premier I think they said, and possibly the lieutenant governor, and certainly the Venerable Nantlais Jones, and indeed everyone who was anyone in St Andrews. People who had missed it, for one reason or another, assured me that they could of course have been there if they had wanted to be, while many of those who did attend were able to compare it with a long line of Algonquin parties extending far back to the days of ladies' maids and private railway cars.

Reports of that function haunted my entire visit to St Andrews. They came to assume a symbolic meaning for me, in fact, because they seemed to give focus to the town's generally more random nostalgia. As a matter of principle St Andrews dotes upon its past. Its most articulate citizens are those most devoted to its traditions, and they are nothing if not steadfast in their attitudes; the pews at All Saints' have been rent-free since the 1920s, but to this day members of the congregation instinctively sit in the seats their families have always occupied.

Two particular periods of local history preoccupy St Andrews patriots. Just as Venetians look back with equal affection to the glories of supremacy and the glamours of decadence, so this town divides its pride between the days of the United Empire Loyalists, who settled this town in 1783, and the days of grandiloquence that followed the foundation of the Algonquin a century later. Both periods are unavoidable in the conversations of the town, and are just as obvious on the ground.

I don't suppose there is a better example anywhere of a late-eighteenth-century colonial seaport — deprived of its ships and yards, but architecturally astonishingly intact. The Calefs, the Pagans, the Maloneys, the Gallops, who moved here across the St Croix River from Maine rather than face life in the American republic, would easily recognize the place today. The streets they decreed are still blessed with fervently royalist names — King Street, Queen Street, Prince of Wales Street, even Princess Royal Street — and are still sheltered by oaks, maples, and even a few surviving elms. Green swards surround the cool white and red-brick houses, some of them floated by resolute monarchists plank by plank across the river from their previous sites. The royal arms still ornament the exquisite courthouse, and side by side along the waterfront are the old premises of the chandlers, the merchants, the tavern-house keepers, and the customs officials.

Grace Helen Mowat pictures the early settlers dressed in powdered wigs, plum-coloured coats, silks, and quilted petticoats, attended by coloured slaves as they tripped up the sands to their new homes. Actually the modest surviving examples of those homesteads seem to suggest that the first citizens of St Andrews did not all live in the aura of mahogany, old silver, and family portraits that Mrs. Mowat suggests. Never mind. Nothing mellows circumstance like the passage of time, aided by the romantic imagination; and whether Charles Briscoe of the early settlers really was an illegitimate son of George IV, whether the Calefs and the Gallops were as well bred as they sound, they certainly built elegantly upon this foreshore, and left a genuine heritage of civility.

I understand the old allure was fading rather, all the same, and the town falling into dilapidation, when the advent of the Algonquin turned St Andrews into a Resort Area, or as the bilingual signs say, a *villégiature*. St Andrews had failed as a railhead and a seaport, being outstripped by Saint John along the coast (the Widow Hoskins had not helped — she had prevented trains coming into town, back in the 1850s, by coating the tracks with goose grease). The tycoons of the railway age, however, knew a good *villégiature* when they saw one, and very soon Canadian Pacific magnates had not only bought the turreted, lawned, tennis-courted and gas-lit hotel but had also built around it a cluster of mansions for themselves. St Andrews became posh in a new kind — "Rank and fashion note at last," exulted the St Andrews *Beacon*, "the gem they long had careless passed." Many a lofty name was thus incised upon the tablets of the town, and to this day we are not allowed to forget them. The Tara Manor Inn (CAA four-star) announces itself as the Former Estate of Sir Charles Tupper and of the Right Honourable the Late C.D. Howe; the nearby Minister's Island is not so much Minister's Island as the Former Property of Sir William Van Horne; a fire station, an academy, and an arena are all named for the late Sir James Dunn, chairman of Algoma Steel, not to mention the auditorium that commemorates Lady Dunn.

It was an experience at once piquant and slightly spooky, I found, to sit in the Algonquin's lounge with one of the more conservative senior citizens of St Andrews talking about the Party and its evocations. As his memories and comparisons reached ever further into the past, the whole place seemed to be peopled by ghosts — ghosts of gracious dowagers flitting through, ghosts of the Ivy League families who used to come summer after summer for their holidays, ghostly giants of commerce or industry, spectral European aristocrats, ministerial shades. . . . As my old friend rambled on I could see them all, clear as daylight, taking tea and scones on the terrace or carrying their rackets among the potted palms and chintzy furniture that in their time had characterized the décor of the resort.

It is not *just* nostalgia. Ghosts they were that we were summoning that day, but in many ways the past is vigorously alive in St Andrews. For the most part those grand mansions are still grand, and the Algonquin, though scarcely the paragon of cosmopolitan swank it is supposed once to have been, is agreeably *haut bourgeois*, and is attended by bellboys in kilts of New Brunswick tartan who lower the flag at sunset to the skirl of bagpipes. Architecturally, the Civic Trust does its fastidious best to fight off solecisms or degradations, whether they be unsuitable conversions or merely inappropriate fenestration. Economically, commercialism (a dirty word among the older of the Old Guard) has been confined almost entirely to the waterfront, where it always was. Light a bonfire on the beach at Indian Point and the Mounties will soon be there to remind you of the bylaws. Speak disrespectfully of the queen of England, and you won't last long in *this* town.

For yes, Empire Loyalism flourishes here still, though it takes some paradoxical turns. Despite its origins St Andrews has always been a half-American town, standing as it does midway between Halifax and Boston, and traditionally attracting rich American summer residents. Its style is pure New England really, its tone is old-school Yankee, and it looks far more happily towards Maine, whence its founders came as outraged refugees, than it does towards the bilingual goings-on of the New Brunswick hinterland. None of this, however, inhibits the royalist fervour of St Andrews, and indeed some of its resident Americans are themselves absolutely to the manner born. Union Jacks fly above their properties, and among the Honorary Wardens of All Saints', a church that greets you the moment you enter its porch with a display of colour photographs celebrating a visit by the Prince and Princess of Wales, is Mr. W. Darrah Kelley III of Connecticut.

I was sitting on the porch of the Shiretown Hotel one

evening when the strains of "God Save the Queen" reached me over my lobster roll; the weekly Kiwanis session was coming to an end, 3,000 miles from Buckingham Palace. I was once about to make a conventional British joke about the honours system when something in the atmosphere warned me not to; sure enough, my hostess's late husband had been a Member of the Order of the British Empire. In St Andrews, two centuries after the American Revolution, *lèse-majesté* is distinctly not the thing, and titles, orders, dignities, and pedigrees are more than mere frippery.

The wealth of this *villégiature*, too, is an unmistakable source of satisfaction. In particular Lady Beaverbrook, latterly widow of the Anglo-Canadian newspaper magnate, but before that wife to Sir James Dunn of the fire station, is spoken of with nothing less than awe. She spends half her time in England, and when she is in New Brunswick lives more or less as a recluse, but she is inescapably present even in her absence. I heard all about her munificent gifts to the town, about her private double-rotored helicopter, about her first-run movies flown in from New York. A woman in a shop confided in me that she knew Lady B's maid — but even as she made the claim she checked herself to add reverentially, "*one* of her maids." I was shown Lady Beaverbrook's house, heavily fenced and topped by a tall kind of radio mast which I took to be something to do with helicopters, or perhaps first-run movies, and after a time, so often was she mentioned, and in tones of such wonder, she began to acquire a mythical quality in my fancy. But then so did many of the other bigwigs, dead or alive, whose names time and again cropped up: I had only vaguely heard of most of them, but they too became figures of heroic legend — Agamemnon the insurance king, as it were, or Gog and Magog who had made their fortunes in lumber.

Few of my informants mentioned the most legendary St Andrews resident of them all, Georges Simenon the novelist, who lived here for a time during the Second World War. But then he drank a lot, maintained a complex *ménage à trois*, knocked off novels with profligate genius, and generally disregarded the message of those Sunday-morning bells. . . .

I heard about Simenon in the end from the town's most distinguished resident littérateur, David Walker, who writes his own novels in a glorious old farmhouse above the St Croix River. For St Andrews does have a proper working present too — not all its inhabitants, by any means, linger permanently in the past. There are no factories in town, but there are three important centres of marine biology, and a famous summer hockey school, and there are hoteliers of course, and shopkeepers, and men who tend the fishing weirs (pronounced "wares," by the way), and Mr. Hatt the scallop man, and teachers, and parsons, and clam-diggers. A freelance entertainer lives here, and a distinguished geographer-turned-merchant, and one or two writers and musicians come and go. St Andrews people like to say that the town comprises four communities: the long-resident townspeople, the summer folk, the marine scientists ("biologues," as they call them here, or fish-doctors), and the newly retired, who often spend their winters in Florida and are thus, I suppose, not one hundred per cent St Andrewites at all.

St Andrews is only nine miles off the main highway, only eighteen from the lively border town of St Stephen, and for all the resistant power of its heritage it has been budged perceptibly by the times. In summer it gets uncomfortably crowded, and even out of season modernity fitfully shows. There is an ugly supermarket on Water Street. An obtrusive motel mars the pleasantly irregular skyline of the shore. The high jinks of the waterfront pub offend some of its neighbours. Some unhappy adaptations have slipped through the mesh of the Civic Trust (ornamentations, too — it is one thing to have a nineteenth-century painted horse above your outhouse, quite another to have a cut-out goose in a bonnet holding a Welcome sign outside your front door). While I was in town there was a public announcement concerning a presentation at the Save-Easy supermarket; it was stentoriously read by the town crier, in full regalia, but when I looked over his shoulder I saw that the supposed parchment from which he was bawling his message had been artificially scorched at the edges, and holed for antique effect. . . .

So the world's corrosion, the world's silliness too, inexorably oozes in. During my stay in St Andrews the district crime story most prominently reported concerned the illicit possession of scaling baskets — plastic receptacles lent to fishermen by American companies strictly for the collection of herring scales (used in the making of nail varnish) but all too often kept in the family as shopping or laundry baskets. I heard of some less specialized mayhem too. There was vandalism in the Loyalist graveyard, a theft from the Sir James Dunn Academy. Supposed Satanists had entered All Saints' Church and altered all the hymn numbers on the boards to the demonic numeral 666. Drugs are not hard to find, I was assured, in this small Arcady, and even as I slept in my bed at the Algonquin itself, some midnight rascal tried to steal a deck chair from the lawn!

Insidiously, too, corruption of a more physical kind creeps in upon these blessed shores of Fundy. One of the most idyllic spots imaginable is that Minister's Island where Van Horne built his mansion, in the heyday of railroadism long ago. It is only just an island, because twice a day the retreating tide reveals a causeway, romantically described on the tourist maps as "a road beneath the ocean." This enables cars to cross, and gave the perceptive knight the best of all worlds, insular and accessible too.

I walked over the causeway one afternoon, and halfway across I stopped to contemplate the scene, and to allow myself a pang of envy — Van Horne certainly knew what he was about. Thickly wooded lay the shores around me, sprinkled with neat white houses, and the waters of the inlet were breathlessly still. Here and there were the shambled sticks of the herring weirs, and in the distance a solitary boat chugged around the point towards St Andrews harbour. The foreshore was rich and slippery with seaweed, littered with dark ponds, and there were ducks around, and some cormorants, and gulls, and birds that looked to me like loons, and a solitary great blue heron haughty in the shallows.

But half the waters I could see had been declared toxically contaminated. The Red Tide poisonous algae was, I knew, creeping along these coasts. Pollution of one kind or another was all around me, even here, and only a mile or two to the north there stood on the foreshore a squalid grey ruin, like something out of a bombing raid: a former fish factory, blown up by the Canadian army as a training exercise and now — dread phrase — awaiting development. Van Horne must be summoning a servant or two, I thought, to turn him in his grave.

Awaiting development! If there is any town on earth that would be the apple of any developer's eye, it is St Andrews, New Brunswick — St Andrews By The Sea, to use the vulgar sobriquet wished upon it by earlier entrepreneurs. Already, like a town expecting bombardment, St Andrews seemed to my brooding eye to be awaiting those same practitioners who have, over the past few decades, transformed the coast of New England from a working seaboard to a Coast of Collectibles. Assembling over there across the river I imagined the whole jumbled army of them — the real-estate ladies and the public-relations smoothies, the antique dealers and the novelty-shop proprietors, the fashioners of driftwood sculpture, the lavender-sachet makers, the Lobster Pot Café proprietors, the souvenir import wholesalers, the creators of theme parks, the property lawyers, the time-share agents, the condominium managers, and the hordes of yuppie camp-followers.

A few scouts have already arrived. Ranging shots have been fired. Already vastly increased taxes are making it hard for small family concerns to flourish on Water Street, opening the way to chains and combines. Only a churl like me would see Maestro Dalvit's estimable festival as the thin end of a Provincetown wedge, but already there are demands for that kiss of death, that last epitome of tourist conquest, a marina. Here as everywhere there are citizens only too willing to kill the goose that has kept them so long in eggs of moderately high-carat gold.

I did not myself meet any of them. It used to be the custom of John Gunther, the great American reporter, to ask of any city he visited: "Who runs this place?" I myself usually ask "Who ought I to feel sorry for in this town?" Sensing however that nobody in St Andrews was really very pathetic (even the old people of the Passamaquoddy Retirement Lodge have their visitors listed in the Saint Croix *Courier*), instead I inquired of everyone, "What's wrong with St Andrews?" A few thought it dead in the winter. One or two young people said there wasn't much to do — but then they would say that of any hometown less stimulating than Manhattan. The vast majority, having recovered from the bluntness of the question (for besides being St Andrewites, they are mostly thoroughgoing Canadians), professed inability to think of anything wrong with the place.

Perhaps they sensed that my question hoped, as some questions did in the Latin language, for such a negative response. The truth is I had found myself perverted by St Andrews. I had responded to it, as it were, out of character. Far from being an Empire Loyalist myself, I would have spat in the teeth of the Pagans and the Maloneys if I had been around in 1783, and I would be ashamed now, if I were a Canadian, to fawn upon the Prince of Wales, or sing the British national anthem after the Kiwanis meeting. My every instinct is hostile to nostalgia, conservatism, the status quo, pedigree, royalty, and all good-old-days rubbish. I think the kilted youths at the Algonquin look simply silly (like all Canadians in kilts, they

32

are the wrong shape), and I despise all name-dropping and what in less genteel burghs than St Andrews they call arse-licking.

Yet something about this little place corrupted me. The truth was, I liked it all. I liked the irrepressible gossip of the old ladies. I liked listening to their preposterous romancing. I was even touched by their reminiscences of the Prince of Wales' visit. (They did up an Algonquin suite specially, but he slept on the royal yacht instead.) I was moved by the innocent beauty of the town, its dreaming spires upon the foreshore breathing, if not any last enchantment of the Middle Ages, at least late beguilements of Toryism and the CPR. Most of all the very anachronism of the place made me feel, just this once, that almost any change would be a change for the worse.

To residents, of course, things are already not what they were — where are they, anywhere on earth? To the stranger's eye, though, St Andrews seems enchantingly frozen in the patterns and postures of its past — a rare survival of quality in the age of trash. It has, of course, several peers along the Atlantic seaboard of North America. Some are just as interesting architecturally, some have settings of equal charm, but not one is so absolutely itself as St Andrews, New Brunswick. From time to time during my stay I tried to envisage what the town would be like if it were to be taken over by the population of its southernmost opposite number, Key West at the tip of Florida. Roistering Hemingway ghosts would replace those genteel shades of Loyalism; the wild rituals of the south, the fire-eaters and the jugglers and the quayside pedlars would be transplanted to St Andrews' more decorous sunsets; an influx of Key West's gifted gays would transform the restaurant scene, and fleets of glitzy sports craft would be moored rank on rank beside Mr. Mered Hatt's scallop boat.

Just occasionally I thought it might all be an improvement, as yet another local worthy instructed me in the municipal origins, or those po-faced Mounties marched down the strand to check the permits of a beach party. But always, just in time, I heard the United Baptist carillon reproachful in my mind's ear.

CHAPTER THREE

MONTREAL

THE *one that got away*

*B*ESIDES BEING UNQUES-
tionably the most exciting of Canadian cities, Montreal is
the most volatile — and the easiest perhaps, for foreigners
to picture. It is the grit, so to speak, in the Canadian oyster,
which may or may not develop into its pearl. I am one of
those who believe that Canada without its French element
would hardly be Canada at all, and I am always moved
by the prospect of the two linguistic groups settling their
hostilities at last and creating a truly bilingual state. At the
same time I am everybody's patriot, and a strong believ-

er in the rights of minority nations, so that by the nature of things a visit to Montreal is an unsettling experience for me.

A stimulating experience, too — "stop any citizen of Montreal," I wrote about the city back in the 1950s, "and he will tell you the story of civilization," and I was impressed in those days by the "bigness and rawness and brawniness of the place." As it happens, when I wrote this later essay, in 1987, the city was in a relatively flaccid condition, the tide of Quebec nationalism being apparently on the turn, and I concerned myself less with the politics of Montreal than with its ineradicable and for my tastes irresistible Frenchness (with excursions into its fading Britishness, too). Since then the nationalist issue has been revived with a vengeance, and my rash prediction that Quebec separatism would never be achieved may yet be rebutted.

On the whole I hope not. I would hate to see Canada come apart, and the dream of the dual nation abandoned; besides, the genius of Montreal seems to me a struggling, indignant, passionate genius, and fulfilment might blunt it.

OVER DINNER AT L'EXpress, a friend of mine drew me an explanatory map of Montreal on our paper tablecloth. It looked all logic, like most such ad hoc diagrams. Vaguely oval in shape, it was neatly divided into street grids and social segments, while arrows here and there demonstrated ethnic trends or economic tendencies. I tore it off when our meal was ended, and took it back to my hotel for reference.

Next day I examined it again, and how different it seemed the morning after! Those handy divisions were far less precise than they had appeared at dinner time, those arrows were altogether less definitive, and enigmatic scribbles, I now noticed, confused the symmetry of the arrangements. What was this about Zouaves? Why was Dorchester crossed out, and Lévesque substituted? Who on earth could Miss Edgar be, and what part of speech, and in what language, was this word Bens?

Nothing looked straightforward, even allowing for the speckles of steak canard around the edges of the map, and this, I have since come to realize, made it a proper index. Wherever we live in the world, we all have a mental image of Montreal as the one big city of Canada that has defied homogenization — The One That Got Away. During the next few days, however, I found it to be rather more, or perhaps slightly less, than that. It is a city, I discovered, that does not quite go to plan. Even its downtown grid system, so confidently abbreviated by my friend's felt tip, seemed at first familiarly like the grids of a hundred other North American cities, but turned out to be an imprint of the ancient land grants which, long before city planning departments were born or one-way streets invented, ran away in parallel plots from the banks of the St Lawrence River.

And what's this at the bottom of the map? Palais des Nains? Palace of *Dwarfs*? Ah yes, I'll be coming to that.

I'll be coming to that. In the meantime out I go looking
for conceptions confirmed, seeking the sensations of
francophonia in what I assumed to be a city of aggressive
Frenchness — the Peppers, I had been led to believe, having
so decisively overcome the Blokes in the battle for its soul.

Smack in the eye they hit me, almost the moment I leave
my hotel, instantly embodied in the holy sites and allusions of
Montreal's Catholicism: the churches on every other corner,
the domes and the spires, the archiepiscopal offices, the
streets named for nuns, saints, or pontiffs, the great grey
seminaries and convents stationed like sombre strongpoints
across the city. Ceaselessly, hour after hour, the pilgrims
ascend in their multitudes to St-Joseph's Oratory — on their
knees up the steps outside if sufficiently inspired, or up the
mesh of elevators that crawl heavily loaded with francophone
piety from level to level within the vast mass of the shrine.
Even Mont-Royal itself, the wooded hill which forms the
eponymous centrepiece of this city, bears itself as a sacred
site, for it is crowned with a gigantic cross of latticed metal
and strewn with cemeteries like a battlefield.

Just what I had expected — this drift of an ancient and
esoteric faith upon the plain Canadian air! It is like the smoke
of an offering, and it issues most dramatically from the Mary,
Queen of the World Cathedral, the metropolitan cathedral of
Montreal. This seems to me one of the absolute buildings of
the Americas — not because it is a miniature reproduction of
St Peter's in Rome, nor even because its atrium is spectacularly
ornamented with back-illuminated portraits of its bishops,
like advertisements outside a photographer's studio, but
because it sits on the edge of Place du Canada (formerly

38

Dominion Square), facing boulevard René Lévesque (lately Dorchester Boulevard) in a posture of allegorical certainty.

Here's the Boer War memorial, and the monument to Robbie Burns the poet. Here's the Sun Life Building (purest imperial classic), and the old Windsor Station (turreted CPR), and the compulsory statue of Sir John A. Macdonald, and the obligatory Henry Moore, that *sine qua non* of civic pride anywhere in North America. A fountain celebrates, like fountains everywhere, Queen Victoria's Diamond Jubilee.

Yet there on the corner stands that cathedral like a masonry glower, outstaring them all, overbearing them all, domed and atriumed, rich in relics and dead prelates, and looking rather like some immense, domineering, and hitherto unidentified beetle.

Behind the Faith, the Culture. At first this too seemed self-evident. Above the river Old Montreal stood much as it did in the old prints, steepled, high-roofed, very French beside its quays, and separated from the modern downtown by a kind of no-man's-land or field of fire. Once a river ran through this declivity, now a sunken freeway, and as I walked across it and the slope of rue St-Urbain to the old streets on the ridge above, I felt I truly was entering a walled city — that I was passing into Nouvelle France itself, that I would meet wimpled nuns and laced seigneurs up there, and find the fleur-de-lis flying above the gates.

The walls have gone, the nuns are wimple-less, the seigneurs are in their boardrooms, and outside the *hôtel de ville* there flies a city flag in which (devised as it was for a visit by the British royal family in 1939) the fleur-de-lis occupies only one-quarter, the others being filled by a rose, a thistle, and a shamrock; yet Vieux Montréal did not disillusion me. Quaint old houses still seemed to me vinous and Gauloisey, lawyers, black-gowned as old Normandy crows, strolled with folded arms through law courts, and there were ships still — real ships — down at the wharves where, 350 years ago, the founders of this city disembarked beneath the flag of France.

"It will remind you of Bordeaux," a know-all had told me, but in fact French Montreal (which now extends, of course, far, far outside those spectral ramparts) reminds me of nowhere but itself. It is a very long time since this was really Nouvelle France, and by now its Frenchness is all its own. Even its faces did not seem to me very French — many looked half-Indian, and many more have been moulded, by cruel winters and unforgiving wind-chill factors, into contours hardly recognizable as European.

Actually, just as all Chinese used to look the same to foreigners, so to me it seemed that the French Montrealers had only two or three faces among the lot of them. One in particular, a plumpish, sallow, but gently sensitive face, seemed to me so universal that at first I thought it was not a generic face at all, but the face of an individual. Wherever I went, I seemed to see this Montrealer. I sat beside him in the Métro. I bought baguettes from her in bakeries. He was there in his thousands — she was too — when I went to watch the Canadiens play at the Forum, and indeed so disoriented had I then become by his inescapable presence that I even began to fancy his quiet grey bespectacled eyes peering out at me through the helmets of those padded giants on the ice.

He suggested to me one of the half-comic figures cartoonists used to employ to represent national characteristics, in the days when it was acceptable to identify national characteristics at all, and if I fancied in him a certain air of communal satisfaction, edging towards complacency, I took it to be because he was now so evidently dominant in the city.

I read a letter in a New York travel magazine, not long ago, describing a visit to Montreal as "a linguistic nightmare." By this the writer meant, of course, that not everything was written or spoken in English. Quebec's Bill 101 certainly wants every public and private sign in the city to be in French only, and the theorists, bureaucrats, and inspectors of francophonism do not relax their vigilance. The tide of separatism may flow less powerfully nowadays, but it has not been reversed, and the Montreal newspapers are still full of its mysteries and debates — is bilingualism common sense or surrender, how long should a referendum be binding, what about free trade, ought Alice Parizeau to have accepted the Order of Canada?

Repeatedly people reminded me about the accomplishments of Quebec nationalism. Hydro-Québec cropped up all the time. Bill 101 was frequently cited. Innocent that I was, I had no way of judging the degree to which Montreal big business has passed from English to French domination, but I was struck by the fact that the delightful Ritz-Carlton Hotel, which seemed to me in the 1960s a very epitome of upper-crust anglo Canada, appeared to have been altogether Frenchified.

All this was the momentum, I supposed, which gave that archetypal French Montrealer his slightly smug composure. I liked him the better for it. I had often been told of his stubbornness, his narrowness, his bigotry; but I took to him anyway, whether he was manifesting himself as an eminent architect lovingly explaining to me the historic development of Montreal, or as the musician Michel Aublet, who, smiling that ubiquitous diffident smile as the crowds surged here and there, played his "Messages d'Amour" all day on his electric organ in the Métro.

Living as I do amidst the sophistication of Cricieth (population c. 2,000) on the northwest coast of Wales, I catch myself sometimes being patronizing about Canadians, but from the moment I stepped into the streets of Montreal I realized that I could feel no glimmer of condescension towards the French of this city. Though one often senses here the presence of simple country communities not far away, represented by the shambling bearded passage of bucolics in lumber jackets, or the somehow wide-eyed eagerness of the downtown shopping crowds, still this is a people whose wiry strength and tenacity is a sophistication of its own.

Besides, it has spontaneous charm: in Canada, as striking an aberration as that peculiar beetle-form of the Mary, Queen of the World Cathedral, over the road from the Burns memorial.

There was an X on my friend's map, I observed, at the place where rue St-Jacques meets rue St-Antoine — a monumental kind of junction it looked, but when I got there I discovered a statue not of a conquerer, a littérateur, or a cardinal-archbishop, but of Louis Cyr, "The Strongest Man of His

Time," all bulging muscles and taut backside above the traffic. As to those improbable Zouaves, I found them in the cathedral; they were Quebec volunteers who fought for the papacy in the wars of the Italian Risorgimento, and they are gratefully remembered in the fane not only by a pair of boots, some medals, and a bugle, but by an epic portrait of their commander urging his men to glory (and certain defeat) over the body of his already incapacitated charger.

An insidious element of surprise, tinged with quiddity, might have warned me not to take Montreal at face value. Who would expect to find, almost opposite Pierre Trudeau's elegantly secessionist sort of house, a Cuban consulate general that looks like a bunker under siege, with high wire fences, video cameras, floodlights, and a Pinkerton's patrol car permanently on watch across the street? Who would have guessed that Richard Burton and Elizabeth Taylor were once married at the Ritz-Carlton? One of the most surprising sights in Montreal when I was in the city this time, was that of the Anglican Christ Church Cathedral, which had been totally undermined for the construction of an underground shopping centre and stood there miraculously supported, steeple, congregation, and all, by only a mesh of steel poles.

And what about that Palais des Nains? This Midgets' Palace on rue Rachel, lavishly refurbished in 1913 by the Count and Countess Philippe Nicol, celebrated midget-stars of Barnum and Bailey Circus, is equipped throughout with minuscule custom-made fittings, from lavatory seat to pianoforte. Its happiest surprise however is this: that as you are courteously shown around you forget that all these objects are small at all, so perfectly proportioned is everything, and so soon do you feel that size is one of life's irrelevancies.

Slowly, slowly up the hill labour Montreal's horse-drawn calèches, on their way to trundle tourists around the paths of Parc Mont-Royal. They are like weird projections of antiquity. Equipped with wheels and runners, like those amphibian aircraft that have wheels as well as floats, their drivers are slumped over their reins, and in severe weather their horses are grotesquely accoutred with bobbled earmuffs, jingling melancholy in the cold.

At the end of the long day they go down the hill again, and if you surreptitiously follow their weary progress home they will lead you to a long concrete building in dockland, ominously close, I am afraid, to the abattoir. The interior of this structure suggests to me a scene not from twentieth-century Canada but from Lvov, say, or Zagreb, a century ago. The poor animals stand hangdog in their stalls, morosely munching their rations and wishing, I dare say, that they had died in glory with the Zouaves, and all around them in the half-light are the strange cluttered shapes of ancient vehicles — high-wheeled barouches painted a Tolstoyan blue and white, heavy old sledges that wolves or brigands might chase, all stacked together hub-to-hub with their shafts arthritically adroop.

The tails of the horses switch desultorily. There is a potent smell of dung, straw, and old leather. A man with a broom emerges from the stables to stare at you suspiciously, but by now you have got the hang of the place: ignoring this serf, wrapping your coat around you, you stalk away as to the manner born towards the building next door — which ought to be the Princes' Club or the State Opera, but is actually a branch office of the department of agriculture.

Boulevard St-Laurent was marked with particular boldness on that dinner-table map. It was, my friend had said, the central thoroughfare of Montreal — The Main — the line which had for generations separated the French from the English in this city of two empires. If, however, I had expected to find Fortnum & Mason on one side of the street, Les Galeries Lafayette on the other, I would have been disappointed: for in fact boulevard St-Laurent has long since outgrown its frontier role, and has become the conduit by which Jews, Italians, Greeks, Lithuanians, Portuguese and a myriad other immigrants have made their way figuratively from the waterfront of hope to the hinterland of fulfilment (defined on my diagram, I see, as Outremont and Hampstead).

This has made the street more or less identical with a thousand others — for where in the Western world is there not a Lebanese restaurant, a Ukrainian baker, a Turkish confectioner cheek by jowl with a Korean greengrocer? Montreal's multi-ethnicity upset my notions rather. I had been thinking strictly in terms of Blokes and Peppers! As it was, Bens proved to be not a part of speech at all but a jolly old Jewish delicatessen ("Thanks for coming in! Thanks for thinking of us!") that might easily be in Manhattan were it not for its bilingual curiosity — "NO FRILLS — NO FUSS — SANS FANTAISIE — SANS CEREMONIE." Half the French restaurants I went to were really Greek, and all along Montreal's trendiest boutique and bistro streets

I found myself pursued by aromas of Iranian cooking oil, Mexican pepper, or Bessarabian garlic.

But here and there as I wandered, just as I had come across those austere seminaries and monasteries of Frenchness, so I encountered ecclesiastical architecture of other kinds — not only actual Gothic churches with porches and notice boards, but churchy *sorts* of buildings, semicollegiate apartment blocks, offices with clerestory windows or early English *portes cochères*. There are few of these buildings in Vieux Montréal, within those ghostly ramparts of New France, but nearer the mountain they dot the streets more confidently.

When I see one I know I am coming home to the British Empire. The Raj arrived late in Montreal, but for a time it was supreme, and it is not dead yet. A hundred thousand English-speakers are said to have abandoned the city in the heyday of Quebec separatism, yet one can still easily spend a day here entirely within the confines of traditional anglo Canada. One can shop, of course, at Eaton's, or The Bay, or Ogilvy's, where promptly at 1:15 p.m. each day Mr. Arthur Dickson the piper does his rounds of the floors, impeccably kilted and sporraned, and tugging at susceptible hearts from Sportswear to Cosmetics. One can wander through McGill University catching emanations of Oxbridge far away, or transport oneself to Platform 1 at Paddington beneath the high glass roof of Windsor Station.

Lunch perhaps, if we have the entrée, at the Mount Stephen Club, a prodigy of tycoon plush, a living museum of that golden square mile of Montreal which once rivalled the consequence of the Catholic Church itself in the wealth and swank of its barons. And in the afternoon, may I suggest a visit to the much-admired school for girls founded in 1909 by Miss Maud Edgar and Miss Mary Cramp, with the help of Sir William Van Horne the railway magnate? Staunchly this admirable institution upholds its motto, *NON NOBIS SED URBI ET ORBI*, and affectionately to their dying days its fortunate alumnae remember their graduation ceremonies in the ballroom of the Ritz, when the pride and beauty of English Montreal displayed itself in virginal white for the approval of its peers. Oh, it is easy enough to think, as the school archivist talks so charmingly about old times and new, as the club secretary welcomes you so urbanely to the stained-glassed, white-napkined, gentry-portraited purlieus of the Mount Stephen Club, that anglo Canada still rules behind the scenes of Montreal.

But no, presently one realizes that this is no longer an Englishry dominant, but an Englishry that has withdrawn, stiff upper lip only slightly quivering, within its social fortifications. Reading the Montreal *Gazette*, which has been expressing anglo views since 1785, I recognized in its often petulant tone the authentic strain of imperial back-to-the-wall, as I used to sense it in about-to-be-lost colonies of the old Empire. The French resurgence has mutated the style of anglo Montreal. Its financial hold upon the city has been broken, and for all the resilience of its institutions, probably its social hold too.

Like those Britons who stayed on when their tropical colonies were lost to the flag — retired generals in India, superannuated planters in Kenya or Malaysia — the anglos of Montreal seem to me to have assumed something of the style of their former subjects. French and semi-French, I note, creeps into their vernacular — one is or is not a *souverainiste*, one shops at a *dépanneur*; I am told that anglophone students at McGill are as likely now to assist at a reunion as they are to attend a meeting, just as they cheerfully obey the Code d'Ethique governing their behaviour in what used to be called Mount Royal Park.

I expect all this perturbs anglo purists — anglo patriots, too — but it rather comforts me. Anglophones of Montreal are far less likely nowadays to belabour me with nostalgic sentiment, or recall their descent from the First Lord Sotheby of Parke Bernet. They are not as shy as most other Canadians. They smile more easily, and perhaps cry more easily too. They are less *numb* than their cousins in Toronto or Vancouver: in short, not to put too fine a point upon it, they are more like the French.

Westmount is the keep of their social castle. When I first visited this carriage-trade enclave, in the 1950s, it felt like an opulently aggressive command post, extending its outposts along the magnificent line of Sherbrooke Street, guarded by the downtown towers of finance, staked everywhere by the mansions of the very rich. In those days such seminarial or conventual blocks as survived in the quarter were like pockets of resistance in occupied territory.

Today a streak of whimsy attends this once haughty domain. One smiles indulgently now to see the remaining manifestations of anglophilia. The cathedral-like structures which once spoke so grandiloquently of financial and social consequence now seem hardly more than endearing fancies: though Miss Edgar and Miss Cramp's school flourishes still, its character raises an affectionate flicker of amusement among the proudest of its graduates — could it *really* be true, they seem to say even to themselves, that we once had a headmistress called Miss Maysie S. McSporran? (They did.) Even the grand clubs are a little comical now, besides being rather empty, and it was a mild joke at the expense of a whole ethos when some wag scrawled beside the supporting scaffolding of the Anglican cathedral, standing there so improbably above its void, the opening line of *Hymns Ancient and Modern*, Number 121, "The Church's one foundation. . . ."

Yet it is not an extinct society, not by any means. It may have lost some of its pomp — and some of its vulgarity, perhaps, siphoned off to Toronto — but it is not without vigour. I could not resist an atavistic tremor of admiration to see that one of the most daunting of those monastic barrack blocks, the former Mother House of the Sisters of Notre-Dame on Sherbrooke itself, is now being reconstructed as Dawson College — oops, Collège Dawson — defined for me by a passerby as "one of our better prep schools." Among the best-known residents of anglo Montreal is Mr. Allan Singer, a rue Sherbrooke stationer who has repeatedly defied the inspectors of Bill 101 — the "tongue-troopers" — by announcing his business only and entirely in English (and whose display of monarchical loyalty, inside the shop, is enough to give the shivers to a Welsh republican, let alone an activist of the Parti Québécois).

And do not suppose that the *French* are undermining Christ Church Cathedral. It is not a papist plot. The dean and the corporation of the cathedral are developing their own alms-generating shopping centre down there beneath the nave, and have already put up an ancillary skyscraper next door — meticulously decorated, in the best anglo Montreal tradition, with intimations of godliness.

They took me to the top of the mountain, and showed me the riches of the city below; but to my embarrassment (for they were very kind) I was not in the least tempted. I thought it looked dispiritingly brown and dingy down there, the city mostly featureless, the landscape around it unenticing. One of the anomalies of Montreal is that it is not very beautiful. It ought to be, but it isn't. It lacks the grand touch, the unmistakable artefact — few are the people in the world who, invited to imagine the look of Montreal, could envisage anything specific at all. It lacks chic, too, whatever its publicists say. Even its most fashionable streets, Crescent Street, rue St-Denis, have a tatty, makeshift look to them, and rue Ste-Catherine, which used to be one of Canada's great shopping thoroughfares, has declined into sad and sometimes squalid mediocrity — its life drained away into the rambling malls which now form almost a second city beneath the downtown surface.

So it is by cameos, not by panoramas, that I shall remember my visit. I shall remember the McGill campus on a bright snowy night, laughing voices from the brightly lit rooms around, a crescent moon, the great cross shining on the mountain above, the glass-and-steel of the commercial city beyond the gates, and silhouetted against an ink-blue sky the fantastic roofs, towers, and pinnacles of academe. I shall remember a room I glimpsed one evening in St-Louis Square, an exhibition, I thought, of franco Canada — so snug, so heavy with lamps and pictures, so velvety-looking in the twilight, as though bombazined aunts lived eternally up there, drinking inexhaustible infusions in antimacassared armchairs.

A shiny man in a peaked cap dances like a leprechaun backwards down a side street, waving on not a party of elves but a garbage truck. A tumble of toboggans gets in a hilarious tangle, all writhing infants and flying scarves, on a snowy slope of Mont-Royal. The night searchlight plays inquiringly, almost apologetically, from the rooftop of Place Ville-Marie. Out on the ice the fishermen sit away Sunday afternoon, folding chairs above their holes, motionless as idols. An old, old gentleman peers very attentively, and a little cautiously, at the winsome baby dolls illustrating the story of Sister Bourgeoys in the church of Notre-Dame-de-Bonsecours.

Frederick Law Olmstead, who created New York's Central Park, brought the same genius for the over-designed lugubrious to Parc Mont-Royal, but he did leave some haunting snatches of woodland up there, undisturbed in the middle of the city to remind us of immensities beyond. And though the bridges of Montreal are hideous one and all, the river they span is breathtakingly evocative, so lordly as it flows past Ile Ste-Hélène, so magnificently inconsolable when it rages through the rapids of Lachine — which are the true *raison d'être* of this city, and which in themselves, I presently came to think, adequately express its meaning.

For yes, I saw in the end, it is above all an inconsolable city — it weeps still for that clash of distant powers which, two centuries ago, first tossed it from empire to empire, culture to culture. It has not, after all, Got Away. When I went to watch the Canadiens that evening I sat next to one of the team's most ferocious fans. She *loved* the Canadiens. "Come on, Brian," she frequently yelled, as a mother to her boys, "watch your rear, get moving, come *on* you guys!" I was puzzled to find however that sometimes she cheered the opposition with equal intensity, and this proved to be because one of the star players of the visiting team was a Montrealer himself.

She could switch her support not exactly at will, but despite herself, and I came to see this ability as symptomatic of her city. I do not mean that its people are fickle or hypocritical, only that history has made them especially vulnerable to crossed aspirations. With the fiercest will in the world it must be difficult to remain an unremitting Quebec separatist in the late 1980s. I know! I am a Welsh separatist myself, dedicated to the independence of Wales from England, and the issues that have animated Montreal during the past thirty years are very familiar to me. We also have a language and a culture to defend against great odds, we think of continental Europe as Montrealers think of the U.S., and we too fluctuate, decade by decade, in conviction, apathy, or despair.

I was sorry, then, but not surprised to find the bite of Montreal's nationalism blunted rather. How I used to love it, when young people in this city angrily declined to speak a word of English — now, speak to them in foreigner's French and they will respond in most helpful anglophonics! Bill 101 may animate the politicians and keep the "tongue-troops" in business, but I suspect it leaves many francophones cold; when I mentioned Mr. Singer to French Canadians, they generally laughed, it seemed to me, with a certain wry sympathy. Gone, for the moment anyway, is the furious beat of protest — I listened for the exaltation of old Quebec songs in student taverns, but heard only M. Aublet's "Messages d'Amour." They tell me that English is all too trendy among the French-Canadian young, and a kind of "Franadian" is palpably developing in the air — how does Bill 101, I wonder, view Club Stan-buy as the name of a travel agency?

In Vieux Montréal one Sunday morning I found myself caught up in a parade. As it happened I was just passing the *hôtel de ville*, whose flambeau was bravely burning beneath the very balcony where Charles de Gaulle once saluted free Quebec. This gave me a fine sovereigniste feeling, and the tap of the drums in front of me, the blare of the trumpets, made me hope that this was French Montreal militantly on the march. Alas, though the parade was French Canadian to the core, and marched with a proud voyageur's strut, it fired me with no fire, for it was only a cultural display: genial people in green carrying snowshoes on their backs, wearing goblin caps with tassels, and interspersed now and then with engagingly maladroit drum majorettes.

The passion has been smudged partly, perhaps, by cosmopolitanism. The Greeks and the Turks, the Italians and the Lebanese — immigrants now provide a fifth of Montreal's population. They have not only made it more like other cities, but have blunted its edges too — even soured it in a sotto voce way. They are reluctant francophones — two out of three of them, we are told, would really prefer to speak English — and they grumble readily to strangers about the French Canadians ("very jealous people," an Iranian told me, "very puffed up"). Far from enhancing the effect of the city, their proliferation has weakened it: multiculturalism in Montreal, I was tempted to think, is eating a travesty of an alien cuisine off a plastic plate in the Faubourg Ste-Catherine. . . .

But far more importantly, it is the very success of Quebec nationalism, transforming the economy of Montreal and making its province so powerful in the affairs of Canada, that has confused the issues of this place. I don't know the French for it, but yuppiedom is here, and the dynamism of Montreal has passed from the Church and the politicians to the industrialists and the financiers. For better or for worse, Montreal has become a complete modern city; the Big Bang syndrome, which is levelling cultures, transcending loyalties throughout the Western world, has even affected this profoundly ideological place.

So nobody has won the battle for Montreal, not even the French — but nobody has lost it either. I fear that the force of this city's pride is fated to settle into permanent dispute, coming and going, flaring and subsiding, advancing and retreating and advancing again down the generations.

Perhaps this makes it more, rather than less interesting as a city — there is nothing more fascinating than an unresolvable cause! Montreal is already the most interesting city in Canada, and for my money is rivalled in the United States, a nation of fathomlessly uninteresting cities, only by New York, Chicago, Boston, and Los Angeles.

As you see, I never did succeed in reducing it to clarity, and perhaps that too — the very failure of my friend's cartography — is a sign of Montreal's stature. It is too rich for tablecloth analysis. Somebody once told me, when I remarked upon the half-deserted sensation of Toronto, that Canadians carry their own emptiness with them, but you could never say that of Montreal. It feels a *full* city, with all the density of texture that a true metropolis requires.

Physically, nevertheless, I found that lack of splendour disconcerting. I pined for vistas, and in the end I found one — at the very last moment, as I walked down the covered way that led me to flight 159 out of town. It was a clear blue winter day — the ground white, the air tingling — and there in the distance I saw a view of Montreal that nobody had prepared me for. It was Mont-Royal from the wrong side — from the northern, wilderness side. On its right flank rose the great dome of St-Joseph's, on its left the tall campanile of Montreal University, and behind them the hill rose humpbacked against the sky. I was seeing Montreal, I told myself, as a Canadian of the interior might see it for the first time, coming to its towers and shrines and venerable streets, its passions and its lofty memories, out of some less complicated town.

It was a high-flown and romantic, if largely illusory view, and I cherished it: for it seems to me that any description of this restless, most lovable, and queerly destined city should end with a heroic prospect.

CHAPTER FOUR

OTTAWA

A *half-imaginary metropolis*

*T*O MANY OF US ELSEWHERE
*in the world Ottawa is less a city than an abstraction.
We have no exact idea where it is, we are sometimes less
than certain whether it is in fact a city, or some kind of
province, and we speak of it not as we might speak of Paris, Beijing, or Buenos Aires but rather as we refer to the
Quai d'Orsay or the Sublime Porte — as a kind of generic or allegory. In our minds pronouncements from Ottawa
issue from some misty iconification of Canada, and am-
bassadors accredited there are simply dispatched at large*

into the expanse of the Great White Land.

This is perhaps all the odder because Ottawa is not one of your invented capitals, like Canberra or Brasilia, built where nothing was before. It was certainly chosen as the nation's centre chiefly because it was more or less equidistant from the rival contenders, but it was a town that had grown organically from functional beginnings. The roots of the place are genuine, its purposes are old, and in writing this essay I detected in the half-imaginary metropolis many another kind of allegory.

AT FIRST, WITH ITS SPIKED and stippled towers above the ice-cold river, Ottawa reminded me of Stockholm. Then on a windy Sunday afternoon I caught the savour of frying potatoes from a a chip wagon in Confederation Square, and was transported for a moment to Aberdeen. And finally I found myself thinking ever and again of Cetinje.

Cetinje? Cetinje was an obscure mountain village of Montenegro until, in the nineteenth century, the princes of that country made it their capital, supplied it with palace and opera house, stately mall and proud memorial, and summoned to it the envoys of the Powers. In no time at all it had legations on every other corner, while its rulers married so successfully into better-known monarchies of Europe, and implanted their personalities so ornately upon the little city, that in the end Cetinje found itself immortalized in *The Prisoner of Zenda* as the capital of that indestructible kingdom, Ruritania.

I am not suggesting, dear me no, that there is any element of comic opera to Ottawa. No capital is more innocent of foolish pomp and feathered panoply (though I must say there is a touch of the Ruritanian to the queerly green-uniformed officers, neither quite soldiers, nor altogether sailors, nor entirely airline stewards, who pour each day in and out of the department of national defence).

But often enough the city seems to me, in its own self-deprecatory way, almost as exotic as Cetinje — almost as deeply in the middle of nowhere, almost as fiction-like in its nuances, just as resolutely equipped with the metropolitan trappings, as well supplied with home-grown heroes, and embellished at least as adequately with halls of government and diplomacy.

Consider, before we go any further, a few improbable facts. In Ottawa mankind ate its first electrically cooked meal. In Ottawa one of the world's first bidirectional elevators takes visitors slightly askew up the parliamentary tower. In Ottawa I was offered one day, without a smile, pears poached in Earl Grey tea. Rideau Street ("Downtown Rideau! Downtown Dynamite!") has climate-controlled walkways.

Ottawa mints the coins of Papua New Guinea. Ottawa is inscribed all over with logos, acronyms, and cabalistic initials and dotted with buildings named for dead knights — the Sir Richard Scott Building, the Sir Guy Carleton Building, the Sir John Carling Building. . . . An eminent prime minister of this capital maintained spiritualist contact with his departed terrier, Pat. The head of state to which Ottawa now owes allegiance lives several thousand miles away across an ocean, but its first presiding authority was the Great Hare of the Ottawa Indians, lop-eared creator of all things.

Isn't it a bit like Ruritania? I felt repeatedly in Ottawa that fantasy, or at least originality, was trying to break through, kept in check always by the Canadian genius for the prosaic; and I was gratified to discover not only that the distinguished Ottawa law firm of Honeywell and Wotherspoon actually lists a partner named E. Montenegrino, but that the Anglican cathedral in Sparks Street, believe it or not, was designed by King Arnoldi. Could anything be more Cetinje than that?

Certainly, for a start, no half-mythical Balkan metropolis was ever more baffling in its arrangements than Ottawa, capital of the most famously logical and sensible of modern states. If you stand exactly in the middle of the Alexandra Bridge, spanning the Ottawa River in the middle of this conurbation, you may experience a decidedly disorienting sensation — may well wonder indeed where in the world you are. Have a care, before you move an inch. Your left foot is certainly subject to the common law familiar to all English-speaking travelers, but in some respects your right foot is subject to strictures of the Napoleonic Code. If a policeman approaches you from the west, to charge you with improper loitering in a public place, he will probably charge you in French; if from the east, to make sure you are not planning acts of sabotage, probably in English.

Several separate legislatures are responsible for your right side, several others care for your left. Three different flags at least are flying all around you, and you stand simultaneously within the mandate, so far as I can make out, of the federal government, the provincial governments of Ontario and Quebec, the National Capital Commission, the regional municipalities of Ottawa-Carleton and Outaouais, the city administrations of Hull and Ottawa, and for all I know half a dozen other boards and commissions that I have never heard of.

Outside Canada I doubt if one educated person in ten thousand could place Ottawa with the remotest degree of accuracy upon a blank map. Most foreigners might just as well do what Queen Victoria is supposed to have done when she chose this singular spot for Canada's capital, namely shut her eyes and stabbed the atlas with a hatpin. Even here on the bridge, if you are anything like me, you may feel hardly the wiser. You seem to be in a kind of extraterritorial limbo, swirled all about by overlapping administrations, rival bureaucracies, ambivalences of geography, politics, the obscurer reaches of history.

Only the reassuring buildings of the Canadian confederacy, whose shape everybody knows from childhood stamp collections, make one moderately certain what city this is.

Actually even the Parliament Buildings have to fight hard to assert their identity on their ridge above the river. When I first came to Ottawa, in the 1950s, they seemed to be unassailable — a stupendous splodge of Victoriana supervising, like some arcane citadel, the homely logging town that lay around. Architecturally Ottawa then was absolutely sui generis, and one came across those astonishing buildings, far, far from any great city, as one might come across pyramids in a desert. They are astonishing still, and the federal centre of Ottawa in all its jagged majesty seems to me still one of the most satisfying of all architectural ensembles. It is however no longer sacrosanct in its uniqueness on its hill, but is invested on all sides, even from across the river, by seige-works of the ordinary.

This is partly just the penalty of national progress — we are in Canada's century, after all. Progress has demeaned Ottawa with most contemporary building clichés. Almost every school of derivative design has had a go at the place, from the Revolving Restaurant Movement to the Academy of Indistinguishable Hotels, to the Mirror Wall Tendency, spoiling all too many views of the wonderful parliamentary silhouette with insensitive height or flat-roofed background. Only the post-modernists, whose skylines at least would be in sympathy with those prodigious old buildings above the river, have not yet arrived. But ironically the blunting of Ottawa has been partly caused by schemes of ennoblement — schemes to turn it into a worthy capital, and to unite its two chief parts, Hull on the Quebec side of the river, Ottawa on the Ontario, into a handsome and cohesive whole.

By its own lights this plan has admirably succeeded. This really does feel like one city now, with the Gatineau Hills as a lovely appendage to the north, and all the symptoms of a modern federal capital are here to see: wide grassy parks with tomfool sculpture in them, pedestrian malls with globular streetlights, jogging lanes, historical markers, and a totem pole presented by the government of British Columbia. There is a purpose-made speakers' corner. There is a garden containing rocks from all the provinces, cartographically laid out. There is a dinky Ottawa Georgetown, New Edinburgh, where nannies and Volvos live. I don't think there are any Japanese cherry trees, but even they have their substitutes in serried rows of that ever-dutiful municipal flower, the tulip.

It is beautifully done, but there has been a price to pay. Just as the Montenegrins turned their heroic mountain village into a poor pastiche of Vienna or St Petersburg, so the Washingtoning of Ottawa has in some sense diminished the place. Year by year the relics of this town's rough-and-ready roots are disappearing. Raffish Hull, where Ottawa's bureaucrats have traditionally gone for liberating evenings out, has been half-obliterated by massive office blocks meant to distribute the capital consequence more equably. Banished from the city centre are the great log jams that used to bring into this capital a romantic breath of the backwoods. The Thompson-Perkins Mill has been anomalously prettied up and turned into a restaurant, and the Carbide Wilson factory is genteelly preserved as a Heritage Ruin.

Even the railways, those sinews of Canadian nationhood, have been cleared away. The terrific Union Station, a stone's throw from Parliament, is now just another conference centre, fitted out, so my guidebook says, with a "triodetic canopy of tinted acrylic." The tracks have been replaced by scenic roads and walkways, the new depot is so far out that hardly anybody can be bothered to go there, and all that is left to remind us of the great trains whose steam whistles once reverberated across Parliament Hill is the faithful old Chateau Laurier, the only grand hotel in Ottawa where you can still open a bedroom window.

But all is not homogenized. Roughage still breaks in! Here and there you can catch a glimpse of what Ottawa was like before the developers and the National Capital Commission got going. Squeezed behind the functionalist ramparts of the Place du Centre, for instance, an irrepressible remnant of old Hull still roisters on. They are talking ominously as I write of curtailing its bar hours, but you can still drink into the small hours over there, as the voyageurs once did, you can still frequent, as Pierre Trudeau liked to, the dance-bars and bistros of the Promenade du Portage, the Lipstick Club still offers *spectacles pour dames* bang opposite the Church of St Bernard de Clairveaux, and the tumbled balconied houses of the backstreets speak evocatively of yesterday's lumberyards and sawmills.

Better still, ever-palpable in Ottawa even now is the immensity of the landscape all around — one of the most monotonous landscapes on earth, but one of the most challenging too. Bears sometimes turn up in Ottawa suburbs, beavers impertinently demolish National Capital Commission trees, the air is pellucid, and from any vantage point you can still see the open country. Only half an hour away are the wooded tracks and lakes of the Gatineau Hills, where the log jams *do* still lie in the Gatineau River; on the very edge of town begin the farmlands of the Ottawa Valley, whose produce you can buy any morning in the Byward Market, just a couple of blocks from the prime minister's office. At least in my fancy the hush of the back country penetrates Ottawa even now: sometimes in the very centre of the city I seem to enter an abrupt inexplicable silence, broken not by the thrum of traffic but only by the swish of forest winds.

63

Best of all, here and there around the capital you may see, as a white fuzz in a distant prospect, as a deafening marvel on the edge of some landscaped park, the fierce white waters — those thrilling hazards of Canada which have haunted the national imagination always, which have meant so much in the history of this wanderers' country, and which remind the stranger still, even when tamed with sightseeing bridges, picnic sites, or explanatory plaques, that this is the capital of the Great Lone Land.

In some ways nothing is more dullening for Ottawa than *being* a capital. It has to reflect the mores, the aspirations, the styles of the country as a whole, and if there is one thing that is debilitating about Canada, it is the feeling that through no fault of its own this nation is neither one thing nor the other.

The British affiliations of Ottawa are fast fading, its citizens keep assuring me, naively supposing that I care twopence one way or the other. You would not know it in the church of St Bartholomew in New Edinburgh, a small and pretty Anglican church which has traditionally been the place of worship of Ottawa's governors general. This seems to me almost as much a shrine of monarchy as a house of God. The governor general has her own crested pew, there are flags and escutcheons everywhere, generals and noblemen are pictured all along the cloister, and there are signed portraits of royal persons, more normally to be found on the lids of grand pianos in ambassadorial residences, at the very portal of the sanctuary itself — as if to demonstrate once more that royalness really is next to godliness.

It is true nevertheless that one feels the old absurdities and sycophancies of anglophilia far less here than in Toronto, say, let alone Victoria. Ottawa is above all a working town — once a lumber town, now a government town — and it has relatively few scions of old Canadian families perpetually rehearsing their bows and curtsies for the next royal visit. Socially it is not, I gather, particularly posh — among the 600 top Canadians listed in *Debrett's Illustrated Guide to the Canadian Establishment* I can find only sixty-three who live in Ottawa, and most of them are merely stationed here. Despite those knighted office blocks there is a strongly republican feeling to this capital: even the royal crests on official buildings, which strike me in Toronto as faintly insulting, do not dismay me in Ottawa, for they seem to be merely expressions of constitutional convenience, besides perceptibly contributing to the Montenegrin ambience.

But if the old spell from the east is waning, the magnetism of the south is inescapable. Directly opposite the front gates of Parliament, like an ever-watchful command post, stands the United States embassy, flag on the roof, iron posts in the sidewalk to discourage suicide drivers who might otherwise be tempted to come careering down the path from the Peace Tower, crashing through the Centennial Flame to explode themselves at the front door. The symbolism of the site is brutal, but not unjust, for there is scarcely a facet of this city, scarcely an attitude, an opinion, a restaurant menu, that is not recognizably affected by the presence of that vast neighbour to the south.

Ottawa first became nationally important as an *un*-American place. The Rideau Canal, around which the town coalesced, was built to give Canada a strategic route beyond the reach of predatory Americans. Today the U.S. seems just down the road — if that. Nowhere in the world, of course, is now insulated against American culture: whether you are in Lima or in Peking, "Dynasty" will find you. In Ottawa, though, there is no escaping the fact that the United States is physically close at hand too, almost in sight, like a huge *deus ex machina* just over the horizon.

Working men in Ottawa have holiday homes in Florida — they call it simply "down south" — and half the people I meet in this city seem to have just come from, or be at that moment about to leave for, Washington, D.C. They suggest to me pilgrims, coming and going always from a shrine, and some of them indeed speak of the experience with a solemnity almost reverential. There are annexationists at large in this town, demanding the union of all North America, there are plenty of apologists for American actions, and in general Ottawa people appear less ready than Torontonians, say, to carp at everything south of the border.

Perhaps they have a more intimate acquaintance with the realities of power; or perhaps they keep always at the backs of their minds the image of that pleasant neoclassical building (architect Cass Gilbert Jr., 1931-32) foursquare and electronically protected at the gates of Parliament.

Not that Ottawans are at all American, still less British. They seem to me by and large quite particularly Canadian — in bearing, in manner, in response.

I went one evening to a public citizenship court, at which newcomers to the city, having completed the necessary preliminaries, were sworn in as Canadian citizens. The occasion provided a climax for a multicultural festival called Homelands '86, and took place in a cavernous echoing hall, like the most gigantic of all parish assembly rooms, beneath the stadium of the Civic Centre.

Was there ever an odder affirmation? At one end the great room was laid out with café tables, and among them Turkish children romped, Croatian musicians rehearsed national melodies, a Tibetan bistro offered brick tea with meat dumplings, and ladies in peasant aprons stood about munching hereditary sandwiches. At the other end, upon a stage, a solitary Mountie in full *Rose Marie* gear provided a lonely and slightly self-conscious element of pageantry, while an almost excessively benign lady dignitary, in gown and white tabs, welcomed the new Canadians to their fulfilment.

One by one those fortunates stepped to the rostrum, to swear allegiance to the monarch-over-the-ocean. The Croatians swung into another verse at the far end of the hall, and the Mountie shifted his weight, poor fellow, surreptitiously from one foot to the other. There were immigrants from fifteen countries, Poland to Hong Kong.

To me it seemed, like all processes of naturalization, somehow a little degrading, but to those actually undergoing the experience it was evidently an occasion of pure delight. There were smiles in every row, and enthusiastic applause came from mathematicians and housewives alike. Eager children examined the documents their parents brought back from the rostrum, which looked to me suspiciously like income tax forms, and when everything was done, and all were, as the lady said, "fully fledged members of our

Canadian family," and the Mountie had stood at the salute
without a tremor throughout the national anthem — when all
the formalities were over, the new citizens settled down with
happy anticipation for the ultimate test of Canadian aptitude,
a multi-ethnic folklore performance.

I laugh at it — I have an ironist's licence, not being Canadian
myself — but I was touched really, and slipping hastily off
before the first clash of Lebanese cymbals, from my heart
wished all those hopeful people well. One of the true
pleasures of Ottawa, actually, is its gentle cosmopolitanism.
Not only is the place full of foreign diplomats both active
and retired (for not a few of them, I am told, cannot
drag themselves away from the scenes of their final *coups
d'histoire*, or at least their last promotions), but nowadays it
is also enriched by ordinary residents of many national origins.
Iranians and Lebanese drive taxis, Haitians clean hotel rooms,
Indians work in Japanese restaurants.

Nearly all of them have been most subtly Ottawized even
when they speak scarcely a word of French or English ("I
recommend this one very hardly," a waiter at Les Saisons
said to me sweetly of the pineapple sorbet). Some acquired
restraint, some special tact or mufflement, marks them out
already as people of this city. If they know one English phrase
at all it is likely to be "No problem," or perhaps "All right."

What is more, Ottawa has gracefully mastered its own indigenous dichotomy. This really is a bicultural capital now.
Government jobs are, they tell me, more or less fairly shared
between French and English speakers; the population of the
capital region properly represents the national proportions.
In the most unlikely quarters you will hear French spoken in

streets, or alternatively English, and in every part of the vast bureaucracy one language seems as acceptable as the other. I hardly heard a single sneer at bilingualism during my stay in Ottawa, and in my favourite restaurant of the region, L'Agaric at Old Chelsea, the waiter and I outdid each other in our determination to arrange for my cod's liver in each other's mother tongue.

I went to the closing night of the Ottawa Book Festival, in the National Library, and found it in many ways like the closing night of any other book festival. There were the usual literary groupies there, the usual lesser celebrities throwing kisses to one another, the usual culturally committed politicians and determinedly enlightened businessmen, the usual plethora of heavily bearded littérateurs (all of whom I wrongly supposed to be Robertson Davies, and one of whom very properly won the poetry prize). To my delight, it turned out to be a biliterary occasion. Two literatures were being honoured side by side. True-blue anglo matrons launched into painstaking French before my eyes, gaunt and furious Québécois relapsed without complaint into English. The winner of the nonfiction prize was one of God's own French Canadians, a handsome, merry, and amiable man who told me he had spent much of his life either in jails or escaping from them, but who did not even bother to inquire if I spoke French — such a relief, I always think, when conversing with francophone bank robbers of literary accomplishment.

Shortly before that event I developed a snivelling cold, and finding myself short of handkerchiefs I took along to the National Library a face flannel instead. What fun it was to observe the good Canadians when, feeling the need to blow my nose, I produced this huge yellow square of absorbent fabric! One or two of them paused for a moment, but only a moment, in their conversation; some could not resist nudging a neighbour; most of them resolutely looked in the opposite direction, willing themselves not to notice. Blowing one's nose with a yellow face flannel is not, it seems, altogether the done thing in Ottawa.

Quite right too — it is not a pretty habit. Still, the reactions of those partygoers did entertainingly illustrate Ottawa's public personality. After a century of capital status, this is still on the face of things a decorous, tentative, discreet, conventional, sensitive, and charming city. It is by no means lacking in fun, but is rather short of panache. Its humour is leisurely. It is very kind. It is incorrigibly modest — *"Ottawa! Why in the world would you want to write about Ottawa?"* — and it bears itself with such careful dignity that even its flags seem to fly undemonstratively.

Of course there is limited room for flamboyance in a city so small. No more than 750,000 people live in the entire National Capital Region — only 300,000 in Ottawa proper. This is the archetypal government town, where almost everything is geared to the exertion of bureaucracy and the acquisition of power. It is obsessed with official matters, speaks habitually in officialese, and subscribes wholeheartedly to official values. "Why are you going to Paris?" a citizen of Ottawa is asked in a local anecdote. "Why would anybody go to Paris? For the OECD meeting, of course!"

Like most company towns, Ottawa is compact and sociable. Within a few square miles everything happens, everyone lives.

I had not been in Ottawa more than a few days before I had rubbed shoulders with the prime minister, the publisher of the *Canadian Encyclopedia*, the British high commissioner, the national librarian, the leader of the New Democratic Party, and the editor of the *Citizen*. I sampled the buffet at the Parliamentary Restaurant. I had lunch at the house where Sir John A. Macdonald died. I took a stroll through the gardens of the governor general's residence, and a man I met purely by chance on Parliament Hill turned out to be the federal M.P. for Ottawa Centre, who invited me to breakfast. The famous in this city are always evident: Margaret Trudeau Kemper can frequently be seen pushing her baby stroller through New Edinburgh, while anyone can walk up to the studio of Karsh of Ottawa, in the Chateau Laurier, and ask to have a picture taken.

Inevitably security is tighter than it used to be, but even now it is mounted in a familial, almost apologetic way. A woman in yellow taking pictures at a political demonstration readily identified herself to me as a member of the RCMP, collecting identity photographs for the files, and her male colleagues from the plain-clothes division, with their gunslinger stances and high CIA-type collars, might just as well have come wearing policemen's helmets. ("You guys are hiding everywhere today," I overheard a uniformed officer tactfully remark to these less than indistinguishable operatives.)

The demonstration, as it happened, turned out to be a very Ottawan spectacle — there is a demonstration every ten minutes on Parliament Hill. This one was protesting against American policies, but with its posters, slogans, and flammable portraits of Ronald Reagan, to be burnt

71

as the climax of the evening, it was not terribly savage, and was easily confined by the police to the opposite side of the street from the United States embassy. When four or five protesters peeled off from the others and tried a flank approach, I heard the following exchange:

Police Inspector: Are you a part of this demonstration, which is forbidden as you know to go any closer to the American embassy?
Protester: No sir, we are just Canadian citizens exercising our right of free movement.
Inspector: Why are you carrying that placard, then?
Protester: Oh, that's simply an expression of my own personal views, as a Canadian citizen.
Inspector: I see. All right, go ahead then.
Protester: Thank you, sir.
Inspector: You're welcome.

So it goes in Ottawa — demonstrators given harmless leeway, police politely defied, confrontation avoided, and free opinion maintained. The protesters went and chanted a few mantras outside the embassy door — *Reagan Reagan is no good, send him back to Hollywood* — and, having made their point, rather effectively I thought, peaceably dispersed.

Can this be all, this common sense, this universal amiability? Surely not. That policeman and that protester probably knew each other from previous engagements, and loathed each other's guts. One must remember that this is the capital of compromise — or of equivocation if you prefer. Canada is permanent compromise, it seems to me. Province must be balanced against province, languages kept in kilter, immigrants smilingly welcomed, protesters warily tolerated. After a few days in Ottawa I began to think that perhaps some recondite accommodation kept this city itself in balance — that some unwritten compact between the prosaic and the fantastic sustained its bland composure.

There are very few overtly crazy people in Ottawa, such as you see cracked by the pressure of more terrible capitals, but I suspect a hidden strain of suppressed eccentricity. They have not been ordinary men, after all, who have made this town. Some have been very odd indeed, and I have come to feel that if Ottawa were ever to relax its self-discipline and its conventions, a surprising gaiety, bravado, and individualism might bubble out, infused I dare say with neurosis. One thinks of Canadians as reserved by nature, but perhaps it is instinct, not temperament, that keeps all things in this country, great and small, so generally even and controlled.

I felt these intuitions strongly at the Laurier House, on Laurier Avenue, for two of the prime ministers who are commemorated there vividly suggest Ottawan opposites. Downstairs practical, predictable, pinstripe values dominate the replica of Lester Pearson's study, in which his personal memorabilia have been assembled. Everything here is orthodox. Here are those vapidly inscribed photographs of international celebrities essential to any statesman's decor, here are the scrolls, the keys, the plaques of esteem, the framed tributes, the robes of honorary degrees and the coloured snapshot of the Lester B. Pearson Tulip. A quick sampling of the bookshelves shows me *The Edmonton Story, The Canadian Dollar, 1945-1962*, and two unsold copies of Mr. Pearson's own *The Four Faces of Peace*. I leave feeling obscurely chastened, as though I have been found guilty of frivolity, and make my way apprehensively up the steep stairs to the living quarters of Mackenzie King, at the top of the house.

But another world is there — another two worlds, actually, for Mackenzie King was of course that prime ministerial spiritualist. At first sight his library seems ordinary enough, easy-going, comfortable, stocked with a couple of thousand agreeably varied books and furnished in a cosy bachelor style. But presently some unexpected features reveal themselves. Around the end of the sofa a dead but still remarkably carnivorous-looking cougar glares malevolently towards the door. On the piano stands the crystal ball through which the prime minister made his excursions into the occult. And in a corner of the room a single red rose in a tall vase stands before a portrait of the statesman's mother, with whom he was also in posthumous contact. The room is rather dark, and should really be dappled with the flickering light of a wood fire: but never mind, Mrs. King's portrait itself seems to my eyes to be sort of phosphorescent, and her bowed white-haired figure casts its own fragile glow across the furniture.

Such a queer old cove on the top floor, such a steady head on the shoulders of the Nobel Prize winner down below! Pearson and King are neighbours in death, too, out in the Gatineau Hills, and there also their contrasting memories seem to reflect an Ottawan compromise. Pearson's memorial is his gravestone in the cemetery above Wakefield, a very boring block of polished stone, without so much as a line of text. King's memorial, on the other hand, is his glorious estate of Kingsmere, with three fine houses on it, and acres of lawn, and splendid wild woodlands, and trails, and waterfalls, and a collection of miscellaneous ruins, from bits of a demolished Ottawa bank to a chunk of the bombed palace of Westminster, artistically disposed among the shrubberies.

I suppose it could be said, actually, that the most interesting thing about Canada is its alliance, whether fortuitous or contrived, between the fearfully dull and the colossally romantic. An entertaining piece in the magazine *Chatelaine* identified sixty reasons why Ottawa's so Awesome. They included Canada Day in Ottawa, Lois 'n' Frima's ice-cream shop, and the prime minister's wife, but actually I think the selection missed the most truly Awesome feature of all: the historical and political mystique of this extraordinary little capital. For myself, I feel it most potently at the northern tip of Victoria Island, which lies in the Ottawa River just below the Supreme Court. I like to walk to the very end of the island, where the National Capital Commission's improvements peter out, and an unkempt patch of gravel and straggly grass looks much as it did, I imagine, when Ottawa was not here at all.

Down there, at inspirational moments, I have sometimes felt an immense and mysterious emanation of power around me, as seers feel energies in the presence of ancient stones. The river rushes urgently by, confused with swirls and eddies — white steam spouts from a power station — traffic streams across the city bridges — behind me is the foam of the rapids, above my head arches the tremendous Canadian sky — and on the bluff to my right stand the central, supreme, and emblematic buildings of one of the world's most enormous countries. They look spectacular up there — such grandly convoluted structures, so gloriously towered and copper-roofed, so exuberantly chimneyed, so elaborately topped with ironwork and flagstaff, so all-of-a-piece but so excitingly diverse, from the Nordic-looking Supreme Court in the south to the great unfinished block of the National Gallery, and the lonely figure of Champlain the explorer on his high knoll above the river.

The force that I feel down there is not exactly political, nor even economic, but something more elemental — an emanation of sheer size and space, of huge rivers and distant mountain ranges, of oceans far away, of illimitable grain fields and awful forests and frozen bays and wild cold islands. Half a continent looks towards Ottawa for its leadership — millions of square miles are centred upon those very buildings on the hill above me — from Niagara to the Northwest Passage the mandate of this city runs. Now that *is* Awesome! Talk about Ruritania!

Maundering in this frame of mind up the road from the island, I dropped in one morning upon the Supreme Court. The cases it was discussing were not very interesting, its judges (two men and a woman) said nothing pithy, the few spectators seemed torpid, the press seats were empty, the room was imposing without being exalting, and I was just about to leave when something astonishing happened. Suddenly the bench was bathed in an ethereal light, not unlike the luminosity of Mrs. King, and simultaneously there appeared on TV screens ranged down the courtroom the figure of a portly attorney in Winnipeg, Manitoba, assuring Their Lordships, Her Ladyship, too, that his client was without doubt, under subsection 22 of the relevant act, entitled to an appeal.

I was witnessing Lex Canadiana — electronic justice, projecting the images of guilt and innocence, truth and falsehood across sixty degrees of longitude to this grey building on the Ottawa bluffs. It was a process, I thought, of truly imperial splendour, and it turned the judges up there, who had until then struck me as a fairly provincial kind of magistracy, into an almost celestial tribune.

And this is the excitement of Parliament, too, just along Wellington Street — its vaultingly transcontinental, ocean-to-ocean range. Simply as a building Parliament is intensely moving. Its library must be one of the most beautiful neogothic chambers anywhere, and its war memorial chapel brings the tears to my susceptible eyes — ah, those battles of long ago, those haunted names of foreign places and chiselled poems of grief —

In Flanders fields the poppies blow
Between the crosses, row on row. . . .

But I was not, to be honest, much stirred by Question Period in the House of Commons. It was a bit like the Supreme Court. Few blazing epithets were slung about, the wit was less rapier than rubber, and the M.P.s all seemed to be on their best behaviour.

In the course of the afternoon, though, a companion in the gallery identified for me, one by one, the antagonists below, and placed them for me in the vast geographical context of Canada. This changed everything. I was forbidden to use my binoculars — "Oh Jesus no," said the guard frankly enough when I asked him — but even so I came to suppose that in the faces down there I could trace all the separate strains of the Canadian identity: pale faces of the wintry north, jaws from the Maritimes, Pacific brows, dark Quebec eyes, Indianified cheekbones, and that particular expression of expecting the best in everyone that I think of as peculiar to Ontario. I heard the varying accents of Canada, too, or thought I did anyway — here a flattened vowel, there a more than usually rotund diphthong, limpid cadence of the West, fervid flow of Montreal. Think of it, I told myself excitedly — the deputy prime minister comes from the Yukon, pretty well in Alaska, the finance minister comes from Newfoundland, more or less in Greenland, many of those parliamentarians down there have to travel for hours and hours before they can even catch an airplane to bring them here, and here we all are in a neogothic palace, in a place that one foreigner in ten thousand, so I read somewhere, could place upon a map!

But I was soon brought back down to earth, or rather back to Ottawa, for now my cicerone drew to my notice a silent and serious figure sitting on a chair below the speaker. Having been crippled by strokes Mr. Stanley Knowles, the senior parliamentarian in the House, has been given the privilege of sitting in that chair, in the heart of that immense political web, for the rest of his life. The sight of him was sobering, but strangely compelling too. He seemed to have been there always, an ageless oracle of Ottawa — last incarnation perhaps of that primeval Hare! He was earnestly following every word, and his head moved from side to side, as though to emphasize that whether the phrases were reaching him from farm or glacier, Atlantic cliff or Pacific creek, whether they were reckless or restrained, wise or foolish, from the left or from the right, in French or in English or in unknown dialect of the tundra, the one response they could be sure of in this city was mute attention.

So I swung here and there, between poles of ennui and surprise, throughout my stay in Ottawa. It was like being torn (in a considerate way, of course) between moods, and it may surprise the more abjectly diffident of Ottawans to hear that my visit ended most distinctly con brio. This is how it happened:

I am by vocation a wandering swank — I love to walk about the places I am describing as though I own them — and it cannot be said that Ottawa is a town for swanking. It is a town, as Thomas D'Arcy McGee once said, for "industrious, contented, moral men." Its Ruritanian aspects never get out of hand, its peculiarities do not generally show, and altogether it is too well-mannered a city for showing off, even to oneself. Besides, when I was there the weather was unusually balmy, making it feel rather less than its most dramatic self, and so even less conducive to delusions of superbia.

But on my very last day in Ottawa the *Citizen* warned us to expect the chilliest day ever experienced for that time of year, in all the recorded annals of the capital's climate. Instantly I sprang out of bed, put on three or four sweaters, and hastened down to the river past the canal locks. Wow, it was cold! I walked briskly along the water's edge, climbed the steps near Queen Victoria's statue, and found myself standing before the great central door of Parliament itself, surveying the awakening city before me.

The sun shone. The flag flew with an altogether unaccustomed flourish. The cold stung my cheeks and sharpened my spirits. And in the glory of the morning, there at the very apex of Canada, a mighty sense of swagger seized me. Down the wide steps I went in shameless pride, and the great tower rose behind me, and the eternal flame awaited me beside the gates, and all along Wellington Street the towers and turrets saluted as I passed. Nothing seemed ordinary now! Cetinje would have stood and cheered! As I paraded that bright icy morning through the streets of Ottawa, whistling all the way and blatantly wiping the drips off my nose with my yellow face flannel, it dawned upon me that if this went on too long, and if I were not extremely careful, I might start getting sentimental about the place.

But fortunately I had to catch a midday flight, so it never came to that.

CHAPTER FIVE

TORONTO

SECOND *prize*

I WROTE THIS ESSAY IN 1984
*to commemorate Toronto's sesquicentennial, a category
of anniversary I had never heard of till then. I had visited the city for the first time, however, during a winter
journey three decades before, and doubtless my later impressions of it were coloured by the half-frozen memories
of my youth.*

*Then it had seemed to me a small provincial city of almost
absurdly British character, rather picturesque I thought, at
least in the snow, given a vast sense of isolation by the*

presence of the iced lake at its feet, given piquancy by a Toronto way of speaking that seemed to me in recollection far quainter and more profoundly Canadian than it was later to become. The streetcars had coal-burning stoves in them. The tallest building was the Royal York, proudly proclaiming itself The Biggest Hotel in the British Common-wealth — or was it Empire? My hosts in the city were delightfully old-school and courteous, and the people at large seemed almost incoherently polite.

By 1984, as this essay demonstrates, the city was transformed, and had become a great Canadian me-tropolis. It has hardly changed less in the years since then, so that much of the piece is out-of-date already. It is an almost instant period piece! Toronto is even more metropolitan now, more Americanized I think and certainly more assertive. I suggest in the essay that in Toronto's sesquicentennial year even the imminent explosion of a nuclear bomb would not induce its citizens to ignore a red light at a pedestrian crossing, but when I was there the other day there were jay-walkers all over the place.

A S I WAITED FOR MY BAGS AT the airport carousel I considered the faces of my fellow arrivals. They mostly looked very, very Canadian. Calm, dis-passionate, patiently they waited there, responding with only the faintest raising of eyebrows or clenching of gloved fin-gers to the loudspeaker's apology for the late delivery of baggage owing to a technical fault, edging gently, almost apologetically inwards when they spotted their possessions emerging from the chute. They looked in complete com- mand of their emotions. They looked well fed, well balanced, well behaved, well intentioned, well organized, and well preserved. Sometimes they spoke to each other in polite monosyllables. Mostly they just waited.

But like a wayward comet through these distinctly fixed stars there staggered ever and again a very different creature: a middle-aged woman in a fur hat and a long coat of faded blue, held together by a leather belt evidently inherited from some earlier ensemble. She was burdened with many pack- ages elaborately stringed, wired, and brown-papered, she had a sheaf of travel documents generally in her hands, sometimes between her teeth, and she never stopped moving, talking, and gesticulating. If she was not hurling questions at those expressionless bystanders in theatrically broken English, she was muttering to herself in unknown tongues, or breaking into sarcastic laughter. Often she dropped things; she got into a terrible mess trying to get a baggage cart out of its stack ("You — must — put — money — in — the — slot." "What is slot? How is carriage coming? Slot? What is slot?"); and when at last she perceived her travelling accoutrements — awful mounds of canvas and split leather — erupting on to the conveyor, like a tank she forced a passage through the immobile Canadians, toppling them left and right or barging them one into another with virtuoso elbow-work.

No, I have not invented her — touched her up a little, perhaps, as I have heightened the characteristics of the others, in the interests not so much of art as of allegory. I

don't know where she came from, whether she was in Canada
to stay or merely to visit her favourite married nephew from
the old country, but she represented for me the archetypal
immigrant: and she was arriving at the emblematic immigrant
destination of the late twentieth century, Toronto, whose
citizens are certainly not all quite so self-restrained as those
passengers at the airport, but which is nevertheless one of
the most highly disciplined and tightly organized cities of
the Western world.

I watched that first confrontation with sympathy for both
sides: and though I lost sight of the lady as we passed through
customs (I suspect she was involved in some fracas there, or
could not undo the knots on her baggage), I often thought of
her as we both of us entered Toronto the Good in its sesque
— sesqua — sesqui — well, you know, its 150th year of official existence.

There are moments when Toronto offers, at least in the
fancy, the black and terrible excitements of immigration
in the heyday of the New World. I woke up the very
next morning to such a transient revelation. A lowering
mist lay over the downtown city, masking the tops of the
great buildings, chopping off the CN Tower like a monstrous
tree trunk; and under the cloud the place seemed to be all
a-steam with white vapours, spouting, streaming with the
wind, or eddying upward to join the darkness above. Lights
shone or flickered through the haze, the ground everywhere
was white with snow, and the spectacle suggested to me
some vast, marvellous, and fearful cauldron, where anything
might happen, where villains and geniuses must walk, where

immediate fortunes were surely to be made, where horribly exploited Serbian seamstresses probably lived in unspeakable slums, and towering manufacturers swaggered in huge fur coats out of gold-plated private railway cars.

The mist cleared, the cloud lifted, even the steam subsided as the first spring weather came, and it was not like that at all. Toronto has come late in life to cosmopolitanism — even when I was first here, in 1954, it seemed to me not much less homogenous than Edinburgh, say — and as a haven of opportunity it is unassertive. No glorious dowager raises her torch over Lake Ontario, summoning those masses yearning to breathe free, and conversely there are no teeming slums or sweatshop ghettos, still less any passionate convictions about new earths and heavens. I heard no trumpet blast, no angel choirs perform, as I took the streetcar downtown.

The promise of Toronto, I presently realized, was promise of a more diffuse, tentative, not to say bewildering kind. On a modest building near the harbourfront I happened to notice the names of those entitled to parking space outside: D. Iannuzzi, P. Iannuzzi, H. McDonald, R. Metcalfe, and F. Muhammad. "What is this place?" I inquired of people passing by. "Multicultural TV," they said, backing away nervously. "Multi-*what* TV?" I said, but they had escaped by then — I had yet to learn that nothing ends a Toronto conversation more quickly than a supplementary question.

Multiculturalism! I had never heard the word before, but I was certainly to hear it again, for it turned out to be the key word, so to speak, to contemporary Toronto. As *ooh-la-la* is to Paris, and *ciao* to Rome, and *nyet* to Moscow, and hey you're looking *great* to Manhattan, so multiculturalism is to Toronto.

85

Far more than any other of the great migratory cities, Toronto is all things to all ethnicities. The melting-pot conception never was popular here, and sometimes I came to feel that Canadian nationality itself was no more than a minor social perquisite, like a driving licence or a spare pair of glasses. Repeatedly I was invited to try the Malaysian vermicelli at Rasa Sayang, the seafood pierogi at the Ukrainian Caravan, or something Vietnamese in Yorkville, but when I ventured to suggest one day that we might eat Canadian, a kindly anxiety crossed my host's brow. "That might be more difficult," he said.

A whole new civic ambience, it seems, has evolved to give some kind of unity to this determined centrifugalism — I never knew what a heritage language was either, until I came to Toronto — but I soon got used to it all. I hardly noticed the street names in Greek, or the crocodiles of school children made up half and half, it seemed, of East and West Indians. I was as shocked as the next Torontonian, three days into the city, to hear a judge tell a disgraced lawyer that he had betrayed not only the standards of his profession but also the trust of the Estonian community. I was not in the least surprised to see a picture of the Azores as a permanent backdrop for a Canadian TV newscast, or to find the ladies and gentlemen of the German club swaying across my screen in full authenticity of comic hats and *Gemütlich*ness. "My son-in-law is Lithuanian," a very WASPish materfamilias remarked to me, but I did not bat an eyelid. "Only on his father's side, I suppose?" "Right, his mother's from Inverness."

But multiculturalism, I discovered, did not mean that Toronto was all brotherly love and folklore. On the contrary,

86

wherever I went I heard talk of internecine rivalries, cross-ethnical vendettas, angry scenes at the Metro Guyanese political rally, competing varieties of pierogi, differing opinions about the Katyn massacre, heated debates over Estonian legitimacy, the Coptic succession, or the fate of the Armenians. There turned out to be a darkly conspiratorial side to multiculturalism. I have never been able to discover any of those writers' hangouts one is told of across the world, where the poets assemble over their beers; but in Toronto I felt one could easily stumble into cafés in which plotters organized distant coups, or swapped heavy anarchist reminiscences. (It costs only twelve dollars to broadcast a thirty-second announcement in Korean on CHIN, Toronto's multilingual radio station: how much, I wondered, as a headstrong nationalist myself, for an inflammatory exhortation in Welsh?)

But actually, this is not the sort of fulfilment I myself wanted of Toronto. I am not very multicultural, and what I chiefly yearned for in this metropolis was the old grandeur of the North, its size and scale and power, its sense of wasteland majesty. Fortunately now and then I found it, in between the Afro-Indian takeaway, the Portuguese cultural centre, and the memorial to the eminent Ukrainian poet in High Park. Here are a few of the signs and symbols which, at intermittent moments, made me feel I was in the capital of the Ice Kingdom:

Names such as Etobicoke, Neepawa Avenue, Air Atonabee, or the terrifically evocative Department of Northern Affairs;

Weekend breaks to go fishing in the frozen lake at Jackson's Point ("All Huts Stove-Heated");

The sculpted reliefs on the walls of the Bay Street postal

office, thrillingly depicting the state of the postal system from smoke-signals and an Indian-chased stagecoach to an Imperial Airways flying-boat and Locomotive 6400;

High-boned faces in the street, speaking to me of Cree or Ojibwa; "Raw and Dressed Skins" in a furrier's window, taking me to forests of fox and beaver;

The great gaunt shapes of the lake freighters at their quays, with huge trucks crawling here and there, and a tug crunching through the melting ice;

The fierce and stylish skating of young bloods on the Nathan Phillips rink, bolder, burlier, faster, and more arrogant than any other skaters anywhere.

And best of all, early one morning I went down to Union Station to watch the transcontinental train come in out of the darkness from Vancouver. Ah, Canada! I knew exactly what to expect of this experience, but still it stirred me: the hiss and rumble of it, the engineers princely in their high cab, the travel-grimed gleam of the sleeper cars — "Excelsior," "Ennishore" — the grey faces peering out of sleeper windows, the proud exhaustion of it all, and the thick tumble of the disembarking passengers, a blur of boots and lumberjackets and hoods and bundled children, clattering down the steps to breakfast, grandma, and Toronto, out of the limitless and magnificent hinterland.

These varied stimuli left me puzzled. What were the intentions of this city? On a wall of the stock exchange, downtown, there is a mural sculpture entitled "Workforce," by Robert Longo: and since it expresses nothing if not resolute purpose, I spent some time contemplating its significance.

Its eight figures, ranging from a stockbroker to what seems to be a female miner, do not look at all happy — the pursuit of happiness, after all, is not written into the Canadian constitution. Nor do they look exactly inspired by some visionary cause: it is true that the armed forces lady in the middle is disturbingly like a Soviet Intourist guide, but no particular ideology seems to be implied. They are marching determinedly, but joylessly, arm-in-arm, upon an undefined objective. Wealth? Fame? Security? The afterlife? I could not decide. Just as, so Toronto itself has taught us, the medium can be the message, so it seemed that for the stock exchange work force the movement was the destination.

Well, do cities have to have destinations? Perhaps not, but most of them do, if it is only a destination in the past, or in the ideal. Toronto seems to me, in time as in emotion, a limbo-city. It is not, like London, England, obsessed with its own history. It is not an act of faith, like Moscow or Manhattan. It has none of Rio's exuberant sense of young identity. It is neither brassily capitalist nor rigidly public sector. It looks forward to no millennium, back to no golden age. It is what it is, and the people in its streets, walking with that steady, tireless, infantry-like pace that is particular to this city, seem on the whole resigned, without either bitterness or exhilaration, to being just what they are.

Among the principal cities of the lost British Empire, Toronto has been one of the most casual (rather than the most ruthless) in discarding the physical remnants of its colonial past. In Sydney, in Melbourne, in Wellington, even in Capetown, not to mention the cities of India, the imperial memorials remain inescapable, sometimes even dominant. In

Toronto they are all but overwhelmed: a lumpish parliament, a university, a statue or two, a mock castle, a few dull buildings forlornly preserved, tea with cream cakes at the Windsor Arms, and on the face of things that's about it. Nobody could possibly mistake this for a British city now: it comes as a queer shock to see the royal coat of arms still above the judge's bench in a Toronto court of law.

On the other hand there is no mistaking this for a city of the United States, either. If that lady at the airport thought she was entering, if only by the back door, the land of the free and the home of the brave, she would be taken aback by the temper of Toronto. Not only do Torontonians constantly snipe at all things American, but this is by no means a place of the clean slate, the fresh start. It is riddled with class and family origin. Humble parentage, wealthy backgrounds, lower-class homes, and upper-class values are staples of Toronto dialogue, and the nature of society is meticulously appraised and classified. Think of buying a house in Gore Vale? Don't, it's twenty-seven per cent service industry employees. Deer Park? Nineteen per cent executive — that's better!

For it is not a free-and-easy, damn-Yankee sort of city — anything but. Even its accents, when they have been flattened out from the Scots, the Finnish, or the Estonian, are oddly muted, made for undertones and surmises rather than certainties and swank. There is no raucous equivalent of Brooklynese, no local cockney wryness: nor will any loud-mouthed Torontonian ocker come sprawling into the café, beer can in hand, to put his feet up on the vacant chair and bemuse you with this year's slang — Sydney has invented a living language all its own, but

90

nobody has written, so far as I know, a dictionary of Torontese.

It is as though some unseen instrument of restraint were keeping all things, even the vernacular, within limits. One could hardly call authority in Toronto Orwellian — it seems without malevolence; but at the same time nobody can possibly ignore it, for it seems to have a finger, or at least an announcement, almost everywhere. Where else could it be said of a work of art, as it says on a plaque beside the Flatiron mural in Toronto, that it was initiated by the city of Toronto and Development Department, Urban Design Group, the project being coordinated by an Arts Administrator? Imagine! "Commissioned by the Chapel Improvement Board of the Holy Vatican, supervised by the Sistine Executive Subcommittee. . . ."

If authority in Toronto is not admonishing you to save energy it is riding about on motorbike sidecars looking for layabouts; if it is not hoisting one flag outside city hall it is hoisting another outside the Ontario parliament; in the middle of shopping streets you find its incongruous offices, and no one but it will sell you a bottle of Scotch. I have heard it address criminals as "sir" ("I'm going to send you to prison, sir, for three months, in the hope that it will teach you a lesson") and say "pardon" to traffic offenders (Offender: "Well, hell, how'm I supposed to get the bloody thing unloaded?" Policeman: "Pardon?"). Yet it is treated by most Torontonians with such respect that if the Bomb itself were to be fizzing at the fuse on King Street, I suspect, they would wait for the lights to change before running for the subway.

Toronto is the capital of the unabsolute. Nothing is utter here, except the winters I suppose, and the marvellous pale expanse of the lake. Nor is much of it crystal clear. To every Toronto generalization there is an exception, a contradiction, or an obfuscation. A kind of cabalistic device, like a spell, tells the baffled stranger the frequency of services on the Harbourfront courtesy bus, and a fine example of the true Toronto style, I thought, was this announcement at the city hall skating rink: "Hours of Operation. Monday through Saturday, 9 a.m. until 10 p.m. Sunday, 9 a.m. until 10 p.m."

What's that again? Sometimes I felt I could never quite get to grips with Toronto. For instance in many ways it appears to the stranger, even now, almost preposterously provincial. Appearances count, conventions apply, theatre-goers attend matinées dressed, if not for weddings, at least for gubernatorial luncheon parties. Toronto critics indulge themselves in childish vitriolics, like undergraduates in university magazines. Toronto preoccupations can be loftily local. (Torontonian: "I suppose you're going to meet William Davis." Me: "Who's William Davis?" Torontonian: "My God. Do you know what I mean when I say 'The Dome'?")

Yet it is not really provincial at all. It is a huge, rich, and splendid city, metropolitan in power — not only much the biggest city in Canada, but a money centre of universal importance. Mighty capitalists reside here! Millions and millions of dollars are stacked! The world's tallest freestanding structure is in this city! The world's largest cinema complex! The world's biggest freshwater yacht club! Mary Pickford was born in Toronto! Insulin was

92

invented! A housewife whose name I forget wrote "I'll Never Smile Again"!

Provincial indeed! No wonder those eight stalwarts of the stock exchange mural, clutching their stethoscopes, their briefcases, and their picks, are marching so irresistibly towards — oh, I was going to suggest the dawn, but I see they're facing west. Towards Spadina Avenue, then.

And why not? Toronto is Toronto and perhaps that is enough. I look out of my window now, on a bright spring afternoon, and what do I see? No Satanic mills, but a city clean, neat, and ordered, built still to a human scale, unhurried and polite. It has all the prerequisites of your modern major city — your revolving restaurants, your Henry Moore statue, your trees with electric lights in them, your gay bars, your outdoor elevators, your atriums, your Sotheby Parke Bernet, your restaurants offering (Glossops on Prince Arthur Avenue) "deep-fried pears stuffed with ripe camembert on a bed of nutmeg-scented spinach." Yet by and large it has escaped the plastic blight of contemporary urbanism, and the squalid dangers too.

Only in Toronto, I think, will a streetcar stop to allow you over a pedestrian crossing — surely one of the most esoteric experiences of travel in the 1980s? Only in Toronto are the subways quite so wholesome, the parks so mugger-less, the children so well behaved (even at the Science Centre, where the temptation to fuse circuits or permanently disorient laser beams must be almost irresistible). Everywhere has its *galleria* nowadays, Singapore to Houston, but none is quite so satisfying as Toronto's Eaton Centre — just like one of the futuristic cities magazine artists liked to depict in the 1930s, except that instead of autogiros passing beneath the bridges, only lovely sculptured birds float down from the high vaulting. . . .

Toronto citizens, who seem to be at once defensively cap-a-pie, as though always expecting you to make fun of them, and relentlessly self-critical, as though afraid you might think them smug, often say that compared with a European city theirs doesn't offer much to *do*. "Oh when I think of Paris," they say, or, "Goodness, when we were in New York we went to a theatre almost every night. . . ." They do not, however, often recall evenings of cultural delight in Brest or Indianapolis. Only the greatest of the world's cities can outclass Toronto's theatres, cinemas, art galleries, and newspapers, the variety of its restaurants, the number of its TV channels, the calibre of its visiting performers. Poets and artists are innumerable, I am assured, and are to be found in those cafés where writers and painters hang out, while over on the Toronto Islands, though permanently threatened by official improvements, a truly bohemian colony still honourably survives, in a late fragrance of the flower people, tightknit, higgledy-piggledy, and attended by many cats in its shacks and snug bungalows.

I spent a morning out there, guided by a genial and gifted littérateur, taking sherry with a charming English lady ("Now you won't be *too* hard on Toronto, will you"), watching the pintail ducks bobbing about the ice and the great grey geese pecking for worms in the grass; and seen from that Indianified sort of foreshore — the city's "soul-kingdom," the poet Robert Sward has suggested — the achievement of Toronto, towering in gold and steel across the water, seemed to me rather marvellous: there on the edge of the wilderness, beside that cold, empty lake, to have raised itself in 150 years from colonial township to metropolis, to have absorbed settlers from half the world, yet to have kept its original mores so recognizable still!

For it is in many ways a conservative, indeed a conservationist achievement. What has *not* happened to Toronto is as remarkable as what *has* happened. It ought by all the odds to be a brilliant, brutal city, but it isn't. Its downtown ought to be vulgar and spectacular, but is actually dignified, well proportioned, and indeed noble. Its sex-and-sin quarters, where the young prostitutes loiter and the rock shops scream, are hardly another Reeperbahn, and the punks and Boy Georges to be seen parading Yonge Street on a Saturday night are downright touching in their bravado, so scrupulously are they ignored.

If "multiculturalism" does not key you in to Toronto, try "traditionalism." It is a potent word too. The Toronto weekend, once notorious for its Presbyterian severity, still seems to me more thoroughly week-endish than most — especially as, having whiled away Saturday morning with the huge weekend editions of the *Globe* and the *Star*, you can lie in on Sunday with the mammoth *New York Times*. The Toronto stock exchange, at least as seen from the visitor's gallery, is marvellously cool and gentlemanly. It costs up to $8,000 to get into the Royal Canadian Yacht Club; the club's two private launches were built in 1898 and 1910 respectively. And though some of the Toronto rich build themselves houses, on the Bridle Path, for instance, of almost unimaginable ostentation, to judge by the realty

advertisements most Torontonians aspire to nothing less
decorous than mock-Tudor, neo-Georgian, or sham-Chateau
— "Gracious, grand and affordable," with elegant libraries,
gourmet kitchens, and "classic fluted columns to punctuate
the expansiveness of sunken conservatories. . . ."

The real achievement of Toronto is to have remained
itself. It says something for the character of this city
that even now, 150 years old, with 300,000 Italian
residents, and 50,000 Greeks, and heaven knows how
many Portuguese, Hungarians, Poles, Latvians, Chileans,
Maltese, Chinese, Finns, with skyscrapers dominating it,
and American TV beamed into every home — with condo-
miniums rising everywhere, and a gigantic hotel dominating
the waterfront, and those cheese-stuffed pears at Glossops —
it says something for Toronto that it can still be defined, by
an elderly English lady over a glass of sherry, with a Manx
cat purring at her feet and a portrait of her late husband on
the sidetable, as "not such a bad old place — don't be too
hard on it!"

So this is the New World! Not such a bad old place! Again, for
myself it is not what I would want of a Promised Land, were
I in need of one, and when I thought of that woman at the
airport, and tried to put myself in her shoes, wherever she
was across the sprawling city, I felt that if fate really were
to make me an immigrant here I might be profoundly unhappy.

Not because Toronto would be unkind to me. It would
be far kinder than New York, say, or even I think Sydney.
It would not leave me to starve in the street, or bankrupt

me with medical bills, or refuse me admittance to discos because I was black. No, it would be a subtler oppression than that — the oppression of reticence. Toronto is the most undemonstrative city I know, and the least inquisitive. The Walkman might be made for it. It swarms with clubs, cliques, and cultural societies, but seems armour-plated against the individual. There are few cities in the world where one can feel, as one walks the streets or rides the subways, for better or for worse, so all alone.

All around me I see those same faces from the airport carousel, so unflustered, so reserved; I caught the eye once of a subway driver, as he rested at his controls for a few moments in the bright lights of the station, waiting for the guard's signal, and never did I see an eye so fathomlessly subdued — not a flicker could I raise in it, not a glint of interest or irritation, before the whistle blew and he disappeared once more into the dark. It takes time, more time than a subway driver has, for the Toronto face, having passed through several stages of suspicion, nervous apprehension, and anxiety to please, to light up in a simple smile. Compulsory lessons in small talk, I sometimes think, might well be added to those school classes in Heritage Languages, and there might usefully be courses too in How to Respond to Casual Remarks in Elevators.

Sometimes I think it is the flatness of the landscape that causes this flattening of the spirit — those interminable suburbs stretching away, that huge plane of the lake, those long grid roads which deprive the place of surprise or intricacy. Sometimes I think it must be the climate, numbing the nerve ends, or even the sheer empty vastness of the Toronto sky, settled so conclusively upon the horizon, wherever you look, unimpeded by hills. Could it be the history of the place, and the deference to authority that restrains the jaywalkers still? Could it be underpopulation; ought there to be a couple of million more people in the city, to give it punch or jostle? Could it be the permanent compromise of Toronto, neither quite this nor altogether that, capitalist but compassionate, American but royalist, multicultural but traditionalist?

Or could it be, I occasionally ask myself, me? This is a city conducive to self-doubt and introspection. It is hard to feel that Torontonians by and large, for all the civic propaganda and guidebook hype, share in any grand satisfaction of the spirit, hard to imagine anyone waking up on a spring morning to cry, "Here I am, here in T.O., thank God for my good fortune!" I asked immigrants of many nationalities if they liked Toronto, and though at first, out of diplomacy or good manners, they nearly all said yes, a few minutes of probing generally found them less than enthusiastic. Why? "Because the people is cold here." "Because these people just mind their own business and make the dollars." "Because the neighbours don't smile and say hullo, how's things." "Because nobody talks, know what I mean?"

Never I note because the citizenry has been unkind, or because the city is unpleasant: only because, in the course of its 150 years of careful progress, so calculated, so civilized, somewhere along the way Toronto lost, or failed to find, the gift of contact or of merriment. I know of nowhere much less merry than the Liquor Control Board retail stores, clinical and disapproving as Wedding Palaces in Leningrad. And even the most naturally merry of the immigrants, the dancing Greeks, the witty Poles, the lyrical Hungarians, somehow seem to have forfeited their *joie de vivre* when they embraced the liberties of this town.

Among the innumerable conveniences of Toronto, which is an extremely convenient city, one of the most attractive is the system of tunnels which lies beneath the downtown streets, and which, with its wonderful bright-lit sequences of stores, cafés, malls, and intersections, is almost a second city in itself. I loved to think of all the warmth and life down there, the passing crowds, the coffee smells, the Muzak, and the clink of cups, when the streets above were half-empty in the rain, or scoured by cold winds; and one of my great pleasures was to wander aimless through those comfortable labyrinths, lulled from one Golden Oldie to the next, surfacing now and then to find myself on an unknown street corner far from home, or all unexpectedly in the lobby of some tremendous bank.

But after a time I came to think of them as escape tunnels. It was not just that they were warm and dry; they had an intimacy to them, a brush of human empathy, a feeling absent from the greater city above our heads. Might it be, I wondered, that down there a new kind of Torontonian was evolving after all, brought to life by the glare of the lights, stripped of inhibition by the press of the crowds, and even perhaps induced to burst into song, or dance a few steps down the escalator, by the beat of the canned music?

"What d'you think?" I asked a friend. "Are they changing the character of Toronto?"

"You must be joking," he replied. "You couldn't do that in a sesquicentury."

He's probably right. Toronto is Toronto, below or above the ground. And you, madame, into whatever obscurely ethnic enclave you vanished, when we parted at the airport that day, have they changed *you* yet? Have they taken you up to Bloor Street to rig you out in mix 'n' match? Have they subdued your peculiar accent? Have they taught you not to push, or talk to yourself, or hurl abuse at officialdom? Are you still refusing to pay that customs charge, or have they persuaded you to fill in the form and be sure to ask for a receipt for tax purposes? Are you happy? Are you homesick? Are you still yourself?

Whatever has happened to you, destiny has not dealt you such a bad hand in bringing you to this city by the lake. You are as free as we mortals can reasonably expect. Streetcars will stop for you, and there are dumplings on your dinner plate and a TV in your living room, if not classic fluted columns in a sunken conservatory. Your heart may not be singing, as you contemplate the presence around you of Toronto the Good, but it should not be sinking either. Cheer up! You have drawn a second prize, I would say, in the Lottario of Life.

CHAPTER SIX

SASKATOON

A *happy surprise*

SASKATOON STRUCK ME AS
*Canada's best surprise. I expected the worst when I
went there for the first time to write this essay. The name
sounded fun but on the map the location looked grim,
and I braced myself for ten days of unrelieved provincialism. Canadians who should have known better commiser-
ated with me, and foreigners thought I must be crazy.*

*It taught me a lesson, rather late in life, about jump-
ing to conclusions, because as you will gather from
the essay, the moment I set foot in Saskatoon I liked*

it. It did not feel provincial at all, but remarkably urbane. Intellectually it was vivacious, physically it was invigorating, and aesthetically I thought it, in certain lights at least, in certain moods, very beautiful.

What's more, though I have visited many other cities since, and written about not a few, the images of Saskatoon remain to this day sharp and vivid in my mind — the sign, I always think, of a genuinely characterful city, besides being a measure of happy recollection.

"OH MY GOD," NEW Yorkers said in their nasal way when I told them where I was off to. "Oh my *God*! Saskatoon! What *is* that? Is that a city, or what?"

The more they said it, the prouder I became of my destination, and the more I enjoyed enunciating its name. Too many Canadian places have prosaic imported names, saints' names, explorers' names, names inherited from Scottish estates, names like Windsor, Regina, or (God help us) Kitchener. The name Saskatoon is in another class. Allegedly derived from the Cree word for a local berry, *misaskwatomin*, it is as indigenous a name as one could wish for, besides being euphonious, exotic, and slightly comical.

It is an all-Canadian name, in fact, and when I got to Saskatoon I found it altogether apposite to the place — almost onomatopoeic. Saskatoon, Saskatchewan, seems to me the most thoroughly Canadian of Canadian cities, the least susceptible to outside stimulants or associations, the most organically itself and in many ways the most graphically illustrative of what we simplistic foreigners like to consider the Canadian character. If I were asked for a topographical allegory of Canada, I think I would choose this very place — the Wonder City (as they called it in its youth), the Hub City (as it became when the railways arrived), the Fastest Growing City on Earth (as it has more than once claimed to be), the City of Bridges (it has seven of them), the city where the *misaskwatomins* grow (and are still made into palatable jams by diligent city loyalists).

At Saskatoon the Canadian sensation reaches an apex, or perhaps a nadir. The Saskatchewan prairie is the widest and flattest of all possible landscapes, and Saskatoon stands uncompromisingly slap in the middle of it, straddling the South Saskatchewan River. The city is governed by the colossal nature of its setting — huge and marvellous skies, unbroken horizons, the suggestion of wildness not so far away, the wide river streaming through, and those interminable scrubby countrysides out there, crawled over by distant freight trains, punctuated by isolated grain elevators and by all too rare notice boards announcing points of interest. Sometimes the cloud formations look tantalizingly like mountains, allowing me to fantasize rocky streams, almond blossoms, and thatched peasant farms, but really there is hardly a bump in the prairie for hundreds of miles.

Saskatoon is a city of some 180,000 souls, extending into the flatlands with neon-lit malls, executive-type housing, and brand new Pentecostal chapels, but it still seems no more than half-urbanized to me. Wild duck, sturgeon, and summer pelicans frequent its river. Thousands of pigeons roost beneath its bridges. Deer, skunk, and foxes penetrate its city limits, and beavers build dams just outside. The climate is intense — ice more than snow, brilliant blue skies more often than not — and the huge northern firmament seems to hang like a discipline over everything the city thinks or does.

On one level this is a farm-town still, where markets are held every Saturday morning in the very heart of downtown, and farm values still count. ("Abe won't be going hunting this year," I heard a lady say in one of the town's smarter coffee houses, and I wondered for a moment if there could be a Saskatoon Quorn, or a pack of staghounds somewhere. Replied her friend, bringing me down to earth: "Well, you've probably got plenty of meat anyway.") At another level the city is the powerhouse of the Saskatchewan hinterland, sustaining the economy of hundreds of thousands of square miles, supplying the finance, the technique, the management, and the communications not just for the wheat fields but for the potash, the uranium, and the gold mines of which it is the custodian and the exploiter. It reminds me sometimes of Aberdeen in Scotland, from whose airfields the helicopters go out night and day to supply the oil rigs of the North Sea; Saskatoon has its own terrestrial ocean, and services island-towns and mine-reefs all over it.

I speak, of course, figuratively: actually there can be few places on the North American continent more distant from any ocean. One afternoon, in a spirit of professional devotion, I paid a visit to the Saskatchewan Agricultural Hall of Fame, an exhibition that, with its massed rows of stolid agricultural portraits, made me feel rather as though I had been exiled to some ideological re-education colony. I was almost mystically uplifted to find in the middle of it a model of an elderly ocean steamship, honoured in Saskatoon no doubt because of its association with the grain trade, but offering my nostalgic sensibility an intoxicating breath of salt air and liberation.

For, while there is a majestic beauty to Saskatoon's lonely pre-eminence, there are cruel oppressions, too. As artists in particular have observed before me, that infinite horizon is a kind of tyranny — one feels that even trying to challenge it, in soaring art or architecture, in soaring spirits even, would be no more than a senseless impertinence. The grandeur of the place strikes me as unresolved, as if it too never quite achieves liftoff, but sinks back always under the sheer hugeness of everything. A schoolgirl put it well in a poem that was published in the Saskatoon *Star-Phoenix* when I was in town. Describing the rising of a moon in that vast sky, Wendy Knippel (Grade 9, Hague High School) said that it rises in golden grace and languor, but when it reaches its apogee it suddenly goes white, as if in apprehension, and simply hangs there, "just hangs there. . . ."

One of the principal downtown streets of Saskatoon is 21st Street East, running from the chateau-style Bessborough Hotel to the modernistic Canadian National building. Along this short thoroughfare, described by one of Saskatoon's fonder memorialists as "an architectural gem," one can see a fair cross section of local society. For a start there is the commonality of the economic and social centre, the bourgeois backbone of Canada, well-fed unremarkable people stepping out of well-kept unremarkable cars: the men, come to think of it, often looking like John Diefenbaker, Saskatoon's most celebrated citizen (he lived in the city for nineteen years), the women managing to give the impression that, while for the moment they are wrapped up against the climate, they will look *much* smarter later in the evening. Then there are a few representatives of the Canadian Establishment, judge-like, director-like, mayor-like persons, emerging comfortable with good food and encouraging commodity prices from the doorway of the Saskatoon Club, number 417, through whose windows one may glimpse, hazed in an aura of privilege or possibly just cigar smoke, ranks of portraits that look, at that distance, remarkably like those in the Agricultural Hall of Fame.

And halfway down the street there is a discount store, the Army and Navy, which offers the stranger less familiar Canadian insights. The building itself has gone down in the world rather — it used to house the much swisher Eaton's — and its customers look, by and large, far less as the world expects Canadians to look. They are not a very affluent clientele. They are dressed, very likely, in rough check jackets, shabby anoraks, scuffed boots. Elderly women wear headscarves and jostle around trays of apparently shop-soiled garments. Children are thickly but drably bundled. There is a fustian air to everything, to the purchasers and to the purchases too, and the faces are varied and often anxious, like faces in a refugee camp.

To an unexpected degree, Saskatoon is a patchwork of rich and poor, rough and smooth. Its history has fluctuated from boom to bust and back again, and its social fabric is correspondingly interwoven. Ample residential streets give way, over a few hundred yards, to houses of elementary simplicity. Noisy young rednecks booze in the bars of four-star hotels. One minute you can be eating stuffed crab in cream sauce at the Ramada Renaissance, the next you can be hanging around the lobby of a bingo hall with the children of the poor — whose parents, within the brightly lit windows of the place, can be seen chain-smoking over plastic cups of coffee, joylessly studying the scorecards and hoping to supplement their welfare benefits.

Wandering these city streets reveals a far richer mixture than maps or statistics suggest. Domed Ukrainian churches, Doukhobor meeting halls, Mennonite restaurants are scattered here and there, while bearded intellectual-looking joggers radiate centrifugally from the University of Saskatchewan above the river. I saw scavengers exploring garbage cans in the early morning, and young Indians offering each other pulls from their cigarettes on street corners. I met, in an unpretentious house on the east side of the river, one of the greatest of living Tibetan scholars, surrounded by wonderful oriental artefacts, with a grand piano and a harpsichord in the front room and a wife enchantingly Viennese. I went to a stage performance of Second World War popular songs, and thought most of the audience itself precisely confirmed the reputation of the Second World War Canadian fighting man — steady, unflappable, not given to false heroics or show-off jitterbugging, just tapping amiable feet to the beat. The old lady immediately beside me, who threw herself with heaving bosom far more joyously into the spirit of things, turned out to have been living in Pomerania throughout the war.

Nearly all these people, it seemed, rich or poor, scholar or scavenger, Scottish, Russian, Cree, or Pomeranian by origin, had something specifically Saskatonian in common. During my ten days in this city I experienced no single instance of unfriendliness — not a single annoyance, in fact — but through all my encounters I felt a mufflement running, a lack of curiosity perhaps, as though the spirit of the populace was kept under wraps. That horizontal tyranny clearly does not suppress the mind — Saskatoon claims to have more PhDs per capita than anywhere else in Canada, is full of lively theatre, and is a very hive of gifted writers. Perhaps, though, it subdues the responses: certainly I found that my own social style, which tends normally towards burbling excess and rodomontade, was distinctly restrained by the ambience.

Hardly had I arrived in the city than I was invited to be a beaver: which is to say, I was invited to put on a hard hat and crawl inside a dummy beaver dam at Beaver Creek Conservation Area, while the recorded voice of an avuncular rodent told me what beaver life was like. I'm not sure if he actually adjured me to be good to other beavers, but that was certainly the tone of his address.

This is a city very skilled at explanatory displays and improving experiences, and its citizenry responds in kind. The children who took me to Beaver Creek meticulously followed the instructions of our guide leaflet as we walked the well-marked trail. ("Gently feel the mosses beside the boardwalk. You'll find they're wet" — and wow! they were!) The adult population waits with unquestioning obedience at pedestrian traffic lights on totally empty streets in the middle of the night — not a car in sight, not a cop nearer than police headquarters. A citizen told me one day why everyone was quite so docile: it was, she said, because it would be so *embarrassing* to be caught breaking the rules.

But it is also, I suspect, an inherited seemliness. Saskatoon began life as a temperance colony and was so well disciplined from the start that laws soon governed even the sidewalk traffic: "Foot passengers meeting one another," decreed By-law 15, 1903, "shall pass to the right, and any foot passenger overtaking another or others shall pass to the right, and any person wilfully offending against this provision shall be liable to the penalties of this By-law. . . ." The taste for order has evidently been endemic ever since. The streets are astonishingly clean. The traffic flows easily along wide, well-planned streets. There are no cockroaches — well, hardly any. During the previous ten months, the police told me, there had been only two murders, and only twenty-six attempted murders, nearly all of them domestic stabbings. You will never be mugged, as you wait there in the small hours for the lights to change, and you must be brazen indeed to spit in Diefenbaker Place or copulate in Kiwanis Park.

Saskatoon also has a powerful instinct for communal duty, communal purpose. The first Saskatonian I talked to, in an airport taxi, was a woman who was about to leave for Nicaragua on a voluntary nursing mission and was worried about the future of her cat; the second Saskatonian I talked to was our taxi driver, who, overhearing our conversation, instantly offered to look after the animal for the next two years. An almost intimate sense of fellowship seems to characterize the city, as you may see from the long and homely obituary notices inserted by the bereaved in the *Star-Phoenix*: "she was an avid bowler all her life"; "eager youngsters would gather to hear his tales of experiences"; or "died Tuesday aged 86 years, 7 months and 7 days." Saskatoon's public institutions are named as often as not for still-living local worthies, and its University Bridge over the South Saskatchewan was designed and largely built by engineers from the university near the end of it.

The Saskatoon Symphony Orchestra, I was assured, could not conceivably close down for lack of funds — its audiences simply would not allow it. The splendid Mendel Art Gallery (which has a civic conservatory attached to it, full of bright flowers and tropic consolation) is not only open for 363 days in every year, twelve hours a day, but attracts an annual attendance almost as great as the entire population of the city. If you build a new house in Saskatoon the city gives you two free trees, to get your garden going, and everywhere there are signs of civic virtue — commemorative plaques erected by social associations or sporting clubs, parks endowed by Kiwanis or Rotary, pamphlets issued by the Saskatoon Environmental Society. At local elections Saskatonians feel something is wrong if the turnout is less than eighty per cent, and city council debates are enthusiastically watched on community television, which seems to me to show a civic responsibility well beyond the call of duty.

"Aw come on," I hear my New Yorkers saying, and it is true that Saskatoon is not perfect. If my first two Saskatonian citizens were almost too good to be true, my first two Saskatonian graffiti offered me a sharp corrective. "A MILLION DEAD COPS" was one, chalked beneath a bench in Kiwanis Park, while I found the other in the main quadrangle of the university: "I HERE [sic] YOU HAVE A BIG COCK." People do get drugged, drunk, or violent in Saskatoon, prostitution is common enough, and one of the sights of the town during my visit was the charred ruin of a house on Avenue J, blown up in mysterious circumstances. If there are no cockroaches, there is no shortage of mosquitoes. The police spokesman on 4th Avenue may assure you, with the sincerest of multicultural smiles, that he is quite particularly fond of Indians, but local Cree speak of constant prejudice, not just among policemen but among the enlightened public, too. "What do I do?" replied my first Saskatoon Indian, when I asked him what he did for a living. "I am a defendant" — he turned out to be a well-known artist, and half the Indian artistic community, he assured me, really was in jail. Time and again, as I marvelled at the immaculate arrangements of this city, I was told how narrow and philistine the civic attitudes really were, how dominated by business motives, how neglectful of heritage. If it weren't for the university, people said, the place would be a cultural desert.

After a happy day or two in Saskatoon I rather resented these flaws and failings. I felt rebuffed. No city is without its seamy side, of course, but in Saskatoon, as indeed in Canada, it seems unfairly incongruous, like a lump in a particularly well-made bed, or slugs in a salad.

Speaking of which, in a lifetime of restaurant food I have seldom eaten more depressingly than in Saskatoon, which

111

claims to have more restaurants per head than any other Canadian city. Saskatonians probably eat magnificently at home, with all that wheat and all those berries, but their restaurants, though astonishingly multi-ethnic, offer regimens of such prosaic monotony, varied in the posher locales by ghastly combinations of steak, seafood, and rich emollients, that by the end of my stay I had withdrawn into a private diet of takeout tacos and preserved ginger.

This, too, is symptomatic of the city, which is in some ways highly sophisticated but in others crudely rough-and-ready. It is cosmopolitan, with its fertile ethnic melange and constant infusion of outsiders, but remarkably introspective. It is one city in Canada that does not seem greatly interested in the affairs of the United States; remarkably little American news appears in the *Star-Phoenix*, though the paper did recently carry an editorial advising the municipality of Pisa to do something about its perilously leaning tower — a safety hazard Saskatoon would never countenance. The British heritage, too, has long since faded here: the only British traditionalist I heard of was the lady who had given the public library a subscription to *The Times* of London, in return for daily photocopies of its crossword puzzle. Saskatoon, it seems, does not greatly care for foreign examples. It aims at an urbanity all its own, all-Canadian (and, like other Canadian cities, I suspect, hates to be thought of as *nice*: a rock singer who appeared in Saskatoon during my stay found herself pilloried in the press as "too sincere").

Physically the place depends for all its charm upon the river, and this Saskatoon has used magnificently. I went to an amateur art show in which an immigrant from Guangzhou had painted the river scene in the scrolled Chinese manner, from some elevated celestial viewpoint, and this ornate vision of the prairie city seemed to me paradoxically proper. The seven bridges do give a noble flourish to Saskatoon, while the river banks have been fastidiously exploited as trail and parkland, unobtrusively equipped with the standard educational displays, and mercifully embellished, as far as I discovered, by only two pieces of sculpture — one depicting a gambolling group of Saskatonian adolescents, some of them upside down, the other depicting a Métis slumped on his horse outside the premises of CJWW Telecable.

Almost everything seems new in this *mise en scène*, and this is hardly surprising, because Saskatoon is one of the most *sudden* of all the world's cities. Until the coming of the railway it was hardly more than a huddle of shacks and tents; the oldest member of the Saskatoon Club (born 1898) predates the city itself (constituted 1906). My Cree friend talked of Louis Riel, Sitting Bull, and his own forebear Speaking Badger as if they were all living in retirement somewhere, and when I was taken to a patch of the university's experimental farm that has been preserved as virgin prairie I found it the easiest thing in the world to imagine its landscape still the Saskatoon norm, buffalo trampling through its berry bushes, bands of Indians filing past.

The early settlers stopped here specifically because of the river, not without doubts — "I don't think there was ever a party coming in," wrote one of them, "that didn't wonder why they had come into this desolate stretch, where they were going and what was the meaning of it all." Saskatoon proved indeed to be a stop-and-go kind of place, going very hard when times were good, stopping abruptly when they were bad, and this half-cock tendency shows. The thirty-odd blocks of downtown display like the rings of a chopped tree the erratic course of the municipal history. Here are the solid red-brick emporiums of the early boom years, the years of Wonder City. Here is the glass and steel of the 1970s, when a spurt in several of Saskatoon's industries made it POW City, meaning the city riding a boom in potash, oil, and wheat. And in between these emblems of success are the symptoms of successive relapses, stores that never quite made it, building lots never built upon, together with the usual jog-along commercial detritus of a middle-sized railway city of the North American West.

Until the 1960s all was given focus by the mesh of railway tracks that represented the real *raison d'être* of the place, with the clanging of bells, the pluming of steam, the wail of whistles, and the snarl of diesels. When Saskatoon's soldiers came home in glory from the Second World War, their victory parade took them from the railway station at one end of 21st Street East to the railway hotel at the other — where else, indeed, in such an allegorically Canadian city? Now the great yards have moved out of town, while the passenger station is away out beyond the suburban malls, and stands there for most of the time forlornly deserted (only two trains pass through each day, and one of them arrives in the small hours). To this day the absence of the yards gives the city centre a sense of lacuna, and deprives it of symbolism.

Beyond the downtown, too, Saskatoon is revealingly layered. Within the inner districts are the thousands of houses built for the most part in the first half of the century. Hardly

114

any two of them are the same, and they constitute an entertaining catalogue of free-enterprise architecture, being embellished with every kind of decorative caprice, equipped with all permutations of gabling, pillaring, shingling, and veranda-ing, and ranging in style from mock-Tudor to the first glimmerings of modernism. Here and there among the residences are onion domes, bell towers, curling rinks, and avant-garde art galleries, not to mention the odd café kept by Vietnamese immigrants and offering cappuccino with borsch and taramasalata.

And beyond these again, ringing the city, are the sprawling malls, industrial estates, and housing developments of contemporary Saskatoon, spawned for the most part in the boom of the 1970s, and only now beginning to show the effects of later retrenchments. Out here is where the action is, where one still feels a sense of pioneering vigour, where the shops are open late and the strip lights flash into the open flatlands. If you really want a sensation of the frontier in Saskatoon, probably the best place of all to go is to the big industrial zone in the northern part of town, which looks as though it has just been off-loaded piecemeal from a container train, and is remarkably like photographs of pioneer Saskatoon in the earliest days of Wonder City.

I suspect, though, that Wonder City was more fun to visit. It was then, before the First World War, that Saskatoon enjoyed its one moment of spree, when just for a few years caution was thrown to the wind, and rogues and visionaries called the city home. Bombast was a prevailing style then, ostentation was acceptable even at the Saskatoon Club, and the first president of the University of Saskatchewan prophesied that by 1931 the province's population would be two million.

Nobody talks like that now. Saskatoon is short on bravado, and, in its social being as in its contemporary architecture, seems anxious not to shock, or even surprise. I would guess that swank is not considered a very desirable quality at the Club nowadays. While all this does not make the city feel disappointed, exactly, it does make it feel a little resigned — like a woman in middle age who, contemplating her husband across the dinner table, realizes without rancour that life's romantic possibilities have come and gone.

But then excitement is not what Saskatoon purveys. It is part of the civic genius — part of the Canadian genius, too — to reduce the heroic to the banal. In his memorial figure in Kinsmen Park, Hugh Cairns, the city's one Victoria Cross holder, is dressed for a game of football, and this is the only place I know in the British Empire that has acclimatized Lutyens's solemn design for a cenotaph by putting a clock in it. Nothing stupendous has lately hit Saskatoon, like the mall that has so galvanized Edmonton. The ever-hopeful city publicists have devised a new municipal cognomen — Success Address — and say that in a new downtown development investors have been invited to "let their entrepreneurial skills run wild." I shall believe that apotheosis, however, when I see it. Ten days of reading the *Star-Phoenix* have taught me to temper expectations. During that time the paper was sponsoring a South American cruise, "sailing between sunny Barbados and lovely Buenos Aires," but I was not surprised to read that escorting the revellers would be the paper's business editor, who would be "leading on-board discussions about economic trends and business developments." Much the most exciting local headline, when I was in town, read: "RABID RAT MOST UNUSUAL, HEALTH OFFICER SAYS."

At the Western Development Museum in Saskatoon a stunning car is displayed. It is a 1959 Cadillac, a prodigious glass-and-finned monster of a car — indeed the most truly prodigious thing in all Saskatoon, I thought, so gargantuan was its size, its opulence, and its frank vulgarity. I stood enthralled by its glitz, and by the thought that some citizen of Saskatoon once flaunted it around this undemonstrative city of the prairies. Was he mocked, I wondered — or was he envied? Did his choice run against the grain of Saskatoon taste, or did it really represent the half-repressed desires of the people, muted yearnings for things more colourful, more shameless, and more abandoned — a cruise, as it were, without the business editor?

One American woman, when I told her I was coming to Saskatoon, did *not* say, "Oh my God!" Instead she said, "There's a song about that place, isn't there?" — and there and then she tried to sing it to me. "Saskatoon, Saskatchewan" was its simple refrain, and it sounded boisterous, jolly, and infectious until, my informant forgetting both words and tune, it petered wistfully out. I had never heard it before, but I remembered her snatch of it, an evasive line of melody, a tantalizing hint of rhythm, as I stood there wondering about the Saskatonians and the fin-tailed Cadillac.

CHAPTER SEVEN

EDMONTON

A *Six-day week*

*I*T WAS COLD, VERY COLD,
when I went to Edmonton to spend a week writing this
essay, and I am perfectly ready to suppose that if I had
been there in the Albertan summer I might have reacted
somewhat differently. However I report only what I feel,
and in Edmonton I felt defeated. I was beaten by the
place. Everyone, without a single exception, was good to
me there. The city seemed to me remarkably handsome.
All my creature comforts were satisfied. I made some

extremely agreeable friends, I was interested in many of the things I was shown, and I much admired the enterprise of people who could build so fine a town in so improbable a location.

I had, in short, nothing whatever to complain about; yet the longer I stayed in the place the more I wondered why on earth anyone would want to live there, and in the end, a day early, I admitted defeat. Forgive me, all you kind Edmontonians! Six days to judge your city! And I probably shan't be back, either.

O<small>N THE FIRST EVENING</small> of my winter week in Edmonton, Alberta, I set out to enjoy a Full Moon Hootenanny in the John Janzen Nature Centre — a friendly gathering around a bonfire, the paper said, to listen for the hootings of owls, and to learn how to hoot oneself. This initial venture into the local culture was a complete failure.

Was there a full moon? There was, but it was totally ob-scured by cloud. Did the companionable glow of the bonfire guide me across the city from my hotel? It did not. Did I hear any owls? Not a hoot of them. Could I find the John Janzen Nature Centre? Could I hell. Round and round I drove my rented Toyota, half-blinded by snow flurries, along unsuspected crescents and down drives apparently unknown to cartography, baffled once to find myself at the intersection of 103rd *Street* and 103rd *Avenue*, stymied by one-way bridges and repeatedly confronted, as I circled helplessly in the gloom, by a sign ominously urging me to REGISTER NOW FOR HOOF CARE CLINIC.

It was an uneasy introduction to the city, like entering limbo, and things were made no easier for me by the intermittent presence, mocking me from the middle distance, of a tantalizingly blazing downtown, a mass of lights packed on a high bluff and fronted by the spectacular illuminated dome of the Alberta Legislature Building. Floodlit baroque and peremptory hoof clinic, hallucinatory streets and unattainable Hootenanny — it was hardly how I had imagined The City of Champions, or, as Edmonton's publicists now like to say, The Official Host City for the Turn of the Century.

It is one of the northernmost big cities on earth, and one of the coldest. On my second day, shrugging off the Hootenanny ignominy of the night before, I set optimistically out to explore the city centre. But this was not altogether a success either. The clouds still lay low over Edmonton, and through them a pale sun glimmered like a very lightly poached egg in a Japanese soup. The streets outside my hotel were half-deserted, only a few cars cautiously negotiating a very slippery Jasper Avenue, interspersed with silently swishing trolley-cars. The subway stations looked disused, so empty were their entrances, and in a small street-corner park music forlornly played over municipal loudspeakers to nobody at all.

Sometimes, in a dream-like way, I was reminded of other places far away. The apartment blocks above the river took me ludicrously back to Beirut above the Mediterranean. The big road up the bluff was a little like Johannesburg. And when I reached the middle of the downtown commercial district I thought at first I might be in Houston, Denver, or almost any other provincial business city of the United States. The Legislature could easily be the capitol of one of the smaller American states (and was in fact American-designed); there was a notable absence of the Anglican ecclesiastical structures, old-school clubs, and royal statues that anchor other Canadian cities in the imperial past; the one unmistakably Canadian building, the venerable railway-baronial Macdonald Hotel, was boarded up.

I thought it a forceful place, even in the muffled winter. The main part of Edmonton stands on the north bank of the magnificent North Saskatchewan River, which cuts a wide white swath through the snow-clad city. The river valley itself, crossed by several bridges, is sufficiently powerful: much of it is given over to parkland, but it contains too the four gleaming glass pyramids of a botanical conservatory, a mesh of roads, and a three-stacked power station that emits white effluent in a rather stately way.

The architecture is predominantly late Bauhaus — few post-modernist tomfooleries have yet impinged — and very handsome too. Here, to my surprise, as I slithered around the sidewalks, was the gleam, strut, and shine of the modern movement at its best, and there is one place in town, at the point where (I need hardly say) 100A Street crosses 101A Avenue, where the opposition of structures large and small, delicate and hulking, half-blocking each other, reflected in each other's masses, seems to me to offer an urban vista of world class.

But there is something evasive and anonymous to it, not American after all, which left me groping in my impressions. The latitude being some fifty–four degrees north, Edmonton's downtown buildings are riddled with the esoteric malls and tunnels familiar to Canadians, partly accounting for those empty streets. But they also include some less conventionally peculiar structures, and these had a perhaps disproportionately confusing effect upon me, like riddles. The foyer of the Citadel Theatre, for instance, was nothing like a theatre at all, but suggested to me a cross between a hot-house and an airship hangar, with a waterfall thrown in. Even more unnervingly, the Edmonton Convention Centre turned out to be a kind of huge hanging garden, spilling down the bluff in a cascade of escalators, fountains, waterfalls, foliage, and exhibition halls, among which were inserted, at one level or another, a couple of restaurants, a Country Music Hall of Fame, and an aviation museum, complete with dangling biplane. I got stuck all alone in a futuristic elevator in this elvish place, and it served me right, for the device was really reserved for the disabled, and I had commandeered it (there being no more deserving clients in sight) simply out of bravado.

"You pressed too many buttons," said Officialdom severely when it came to rescue me, but Officialdom was wrong — I had pressed only the one. I did not argue, however, for with some relief I recognized in this veiled reproach the authentic voice of Canada.

My third day in Edmonton I consecrated to Canadianness. I ignored that equivocal downtown and went instead to the unmistakably indigenous quarter of Strathcona, whose very name struck me as allegorically of the country. When the railway first came up here from Calgary it stopped south of the river, and there grew up around its terminus — the End of Steel — an archetypal prairie settlement of the nineteenth century. It is recognizable still, and offers a homely contrast to the skyscraper clump over the way.

The freight trains still come to Strathcona, the tracks still sprawl there, and beyond it (although in fact mile after mile of suburbia extends to the south) one can fancy the farmlands running away flat as a table to the horizon. In the way of such communities it has been slightly tarted up with sham gaslights and craft shops: "Ciao babe," I heard one girl say to another in one of its cafés, and "Yah," her friend replied. Nevertheless its main street still *feels* like a main street, with a grand old hotel, and a theatre, a car dealer or two, the Coin Castle pinball arcade, and a fast-food shop offering HHHOT DOGS 2 FOR 99 ¢ . At a pinch, if you ignore Veggies (Concepts in Vegetarian Cuisine) and the Divinely Decadent clothes store, you can still imagine the days when the newsboys sold *The Homesteader* on Whyte Avenue, and the snort and wail of the steam trains brought the railwaymen tumbling from the Strathcona Hotel tavern.

It offered me, though, no rumbustious vibrations. I don't think those railwaymen would have been very bawdy, for I sense an inherited strain of reserve to the Canadianness of Edmonton. The city swarms with every kind of foreign incomer — the public library offers books in Chinese, Japanese, Vietnamese, Gujerati, Urdu, and Korean, and the

first dish I ate in Edmonton was mushroom strudel with as-
paragus. Yet it does not feel in the least like an immigrant
city, perhaps because it was cosmopolitan almost from the
start, with a long-established francophone community, and
was never one of your true-blue stuck-up towns of the English
ascendancy. Even the few Indians I saw at least *looked* more
integrated than most, and I found it hard to realize that only
a few generations ago, within the very purlieus of this place,
Cree and Blackfoot lived in tribal panoply, pitching their tents
on Whyte Avenue sometimes, fighting occasional battles and
dancing the Sun Dance with full mystery of Sacred Turnip,
Bear Pigeon Society, and Holy Virtuous Woman.

The Canadianness of the place worked on me rather slyly.
There were the destination names down at the Greyhound
Bus Station (Wandering River, Elk Point, Red Deer, and
Rocky Mountain House). There were the gentle originals I
encountered here and there — the merry deaf-and-dumb boy
who directed me to Eaton's — the street-corner evangelist
shouting his exhortations into the driving snow like an
auctioneer or a race commentator — the sweetly eccentric
old lady in the bookshop ending her every sentence with a
little musical phrase in a high girlish voice, like the call of
a lemur.

There was the distinguished filmmaker, too, whose
grandfather had actually founded *The Homesteader*, and
whose mother had attended the inaugural banquet of the
poor old Macdonald Hotel. There was the eminent academic
whose specialty was mission history in the Canadian West,
who knew all there was to know about gardening in Alberta,
and whose wife gave me a loaf of home-made bread to cheer

up my hotel breakfast. There was the celebrated publisher, the first major Canadian publisher to defy the supremacy of the East, who lived in a superb log house above the river, and who drove me home in his Jaguar with his two dogs, the majestic Oliver and the petite Victoria, poking their heads out of the rear window into the freezing wind.

And the view from my own window was Canadian in a distinctly insidious way: the Great West Saddlery Co. Ltd., Café Budapest, W.C. Kay the Gold and Gem Merchants, the gentrified Boardwalk Market decorated with fairy lights, stacked office towers beyond, and the illuminated thermometer, on a building across the street, registering minus twenty-three degrees centigrade.

The snow fell, and all night long the snowploughs clanked and scraped outside my window. My fourth day in Edmonton, though, dawned splendidly. The city was white and silvery, the sky was an icy blue, and from the tall downtown towers, from the refinery chimneys on the distant horizon, from the power station in the river valley, driven plumes of steam, billowing in parallel before the wind, gave the whole scene a touch of grandiloquence.

Grandiloquent, however, Edmonton generally isn't. Indeed most of the city's claims about itself are disarmingly modest, in the biggest-west-of-Winnipeg mode. I was beguiled to read that the Edmonton Police Department's Pipe Band is "the only one in the world authorized to wear the badges of two serving regiments" — no! I was touched to discover, in a list of significant dates in local history, the following entry for the year 1874: "NWMP Did Not Settle Here." There are doubtless epic tales to be told about Edmonton's pioneers, prospectors, entrepreneurs, and hockey players, but the obvious civic candidate for a place in the *Guinness Book of World Records* is Edmonton's most famous institution (Oilers apart), the West Edmonton Mall. Having heard it vilified by almost all my informants, I thought this splendid glittery day a good time to judge it for myself.

But how can one judge "the World's Largest Fun, Fashion and Entertainment Centre?" It is heaven, hell, and purgatory. It is performing beasts and captive pheasants, the Alberta Baroque Ensemble on a Sunday afternoon, nineteen cinemas, 800 shops including half a dozen of the best stores in Canada, 110 eating-houses, an indoor eighteen-hole golf course, electric scooters for rent, and the Fantasyland Hotel.

I would do almost anything rather than experience for myself the Mindbender Rollercoaster or the thirteen-storey Drop of Doom in the World's Largest Indoor Amusement Park. I would rather eat bread and water than dine in any of the restaurants in the popcorn-fragrant Gourmet Court. I cast a curse upon the owners of the West Edmonton Mall for their barbaric imprisonment of those beautiful birds, and their wicked exploitation of dolphins.

On the other hand I know few more charming sights than that of the infant Edmontonians in their many-coloured crash-helmets learning to skate at the Ice Palace, watched by their doting parents — bright as buttons, bouncy as balls, often surprisingly graceful and frequently very funny. I am greatly entertained by the submarine fleet in the Deep Sea Adventure ("more submarines than the Canadian Navy"), and in a Grand Guignol way I find the Mindbender and the Drop of Doom spellbinding to watch. I quite like wandering the shopping arcades, which offer not only cars for sale, replicas of the British crown jewels, and a family medical centre seven days a week, but also three or four good bookshops. I am genuinely amazed at the gigantic glass-roofed Waterpark, like a bottled slice of a beach somewhere, where waves roll, the sun permanently shines, and women in bikinis really do sunbathe on the foreshore.

Somebody told me the West Edmonton Mall aimed at an average mental age of nine, but I don't think age really comes into it. This prodigy is geared rather to a taste — the taste of the age, which is shared, if in different quantities, by nearly all of us. Entirely indoors, mostly artificial, largely derivative, it is a very declaration of contemporary capitalism, the world-conquering ideology of our time. It is beyond nationality, beyond pretension actually, and however much you may detest it yourself, you must be a sourpuss indeed to resist the eager excitement in the faces of people young and old, for better or for worse, as they enter its shameless enclave.

At least it is explicit. Could it perhaps be, I began to wonder as my fourth day came to an end, that this fantasy was the one thing in Edmonton that I had really got the hang of?

For the rest of the city seemed to be losing, rather than gaining, clarity in my mind. I could find no figure for it, even after five days. It is a city of many flags, but they look oddly out of place, so indeterminate does the civic message seem to be. Edmonton has few instantly recognizable features, and so far as I could see no very pronounced local characteristics. People did not talk in a recognizably Edmonton way, or cook specifically Edmonton dishes. I suspected that even the most vividly exotic faces, peering back at me over sushi counters or Mongolian barbecues, would presently be homogenized by usage and climate. I noticed very few striking-looking people in Edmonton, and in everyday intercourse with strangers I heard nobody say a single unexpected thing (unless you count the snowstorm evangelist, the melodious book-buyer, and the eloquent deaf-mute).

Sometimes I thought it the least Canadian of cities, in its lack of icons or traditions. I never did discover where the lieutenant governor of Alberta lived, I came across no tributes to the Fathers of Confederation, and the present mayor of Edmonton admirably declines to wear the mayoral scarf of office because it is made of beaver pelts. At other times I thought it the most Canadian of cities, but of an indistinct kind. I had expected it to stand, temperamentally speaking, somewhere between Saskatoon and Calgary, but in the end I concluded its character to be altogether unique.

For one thing, despite a downtown that has mostly erupted during the past twenty years, despite my friend's mother's clear memory of the inaugural dinner at the Macdonald Hotel, Edmonton does not feel a young city. There is nothing brash about it, except that mall, of course, and in winter anyway its style is steady and considered. It seemed to me a gradualist kind of place. People have been settled on its site since the 1790s, when the fur men erected their first fort on the river bluff — long before the trains arrived, the York boats, and after them the paddle-steamers, were coming and going up the river.

Since then Edmonton appears to have developed, through

many a boom and many a bust, with persistent *reasonable-ness*. For years, before the trains came, it was more on its own than most Canadian cities, and the communal cohesion still shows. Snow smudged all its edges when I was there, but it seemed to me that one part of Edmonton ran easily enough into the next, rich Jasper Avenue easing itself into the shabby eastern outskirts, the silver dome of the Russian cathedral shining congruously enough through the modernistic windows of the Convention Centre. Most of the University of Alberta's buildings look more or less indistinguishable from the apartment blocks and office towers around, and there is no very dramatic contrast between the simple frame house in which my publisher friend had been born and the riverside villa, a couple of blocks away, in which he and his wife are now guarded among their books and pictures by Oliver and Victoria.

Perhaps all this is because Edmonton has always been a liberal city. It is a place of bureaucrats and academics — the university is the second largest in all Canada. Theatres abound. Art galleries are two a penny. Bookshops are nearly always within reach. The natural history dioramas in the provincial museum are the best I have ever seen. A professional symphony orchestra flourishes, there are several publishing houses, the Edmonton *Journal* isn't bad, and there is a lively film industry. They tell me the annual Fringe Festival is terrific. For a city of its size Edmonton is cultivated not just by North American but by European standards.

And yet it left me curiously indifferent — not cold exactly, except in a physical sense, but unengaged. It never grabbed me. If I was disoriented that first evening, as I searched in vain for the Hootenanny, I had found no clearer course five days later as I hunted for civic meanings. The Official Host City had opened its doors graciously indeed, but for the life of me I could not make out what there was inside.

The cold wore on. That thermometer outside my window hovered around the middle twenties below zero. When I returned from a walk I felt like Titus Oates. How could the Edmontonians stand it, I wondered, for a whole winter — or a whole lifetime? Was it only to strangers that the city seemed so bewilderingly unresolved, or did its citizens too feel their navigations vague? So flat, so far away, so bitter half the year — what profits or pleasures could compensate for the disadvantages of Edmonton?

That they *do* compensate seems, even among the proudest citizens, to be at best a matter of love or faith, at worst a matter of will; and for myself, though I discovered very little unpleasant in Edmonton, and saw much to admire, and enjoyed nothing but generous kindness from the inhabitants, still I never did complete my winter week there after all. "Edmonton," a colleague in Toronto had told me, "will be a challenge to you," and he was right. Edmonton beat me, in fact. On the sixth day my spirit failed, and I crept away ashamed.

CHAPTER EIGHT

BANFF

WHISTLE *stop*

*T*HIS LITTLE PIECE TURNS out to be an exercise in nostalgia, for it commemorates a traditional Canadian delight no longer available — a stop-off in Banff in the course of a transcontinental train journey. The images of this pleasure are, to the world at large, among the most familiar of all Canadian metaphors: with the Mounties, perhaps, and possibly Parliament Hill in Ottawa, nothing has spoken more familiarly of Canada than the vision of the great passenger train sweeping out *of the snows into the little mountain town, and the lordly splendour of the railway hotel which was for so many generations an essential part of the Canadian mystique. Not so long after I wrote the essay transcontinental service through Banff came to an end, and never again can anyone enjoy the old thrill that I experienced, when the train dropped me off at Banff that evening, and picked me up for Vancouver next day.*

IN FORMER TIMES THE SWELLS of the Western world, taking a train ride across Canada from one ocean to the next, liked to stop off at Banff, in the heart of the Alberta Rockies, where the Canadian Pacific Railway had built for their convenience one of the great hotels of the North American continent, in one of the most astonishing mountain sites on earth.

The trains still run, though the toffs are rarer nowadays; the Banff Springs Hotel still flourishes, though one could hardly call it one of North America's greatest; the scene is still spectacular, though a hundred thousand pictures have somewhat diminished its power to amaze; and so one winter day, travelling on VIA Train 001 to Vancouver, I decided to do what the *beau monde* used to do, and give myself twenty-four hours in Banff, Alberta.

Jingling horse-drawn sleighs used to meet the old steam trains. A friend of mine met me with his Saab instead, but still we drove away from the depot, up the slithery main street of the

little town, in a perceptibly festive manner. Banff is nothing
if not for fun. The train from the east arrives in the early evening, just as the dusk sets in, and the lights of the
town were already bright against the snow as my companion displayed for me, *en passant*, the modest but beguiling
urban sights.

Some of these were more or less what I expected. There
was the museum, a little delight in a kind of Victorian Lap-
land architecture, and there were the requisitely assorted
churches, and a few fairly glitzy new motels. The Hudson's
Bay Company store was there, of course, on Banff Avenue,
and I noted without surprise that the Grizzly Restaurant was
serving not only buffalo steaks but caribou too. On the other hand I was rather taken aback, as my predecessors of the
steam age would certainly have been, by the Mediterranean
dazzle of the Balkan Restaurant (excellent retsina, my friend
told me), and the evident suavity of Le Beaujolais (cost you
a packet, he said). I had not expected to find half the milling tourists Japanese, and half the novelty shops apparently
Japanese-owned. And how odd it was to observe, here in the
anglo-Canadian fastnesses of Alberta, that every single traffic
sign was bilingual — the place being in a national park, Canadian federal laws applied.

Banff is hardly more than a village, for all its celebrity.
Very soon we saw rising above us, as we crossed the frozen river, the immense reddish pile of the hotel, palace-
like still, its tower and high gabled roofs in grandiloquent
silhouette against the forests and white mountains behind. It
looked precisely as the old globetrotters must have seen it,
wrapping their elk-skin rugs around their knees and debating

whether to wear the chiffon or the *crêpe-de-chine* for dinner.

Urbanity is no longer evident among the stupendous shabby grandeurs of the hotel, but at least its clientele remains vividly cosmopolitan. The Japanese have their own tour desk there, and when we went to the coffee shop we found it crowded with vivacious young people from all over. Banff is full of resident un-Canadians, semi-Canadians, and would-be Canadians, Australians most noticeably (but then they are always most noticeable) — some working at the Banff Centre down the road from the hotel, some I gathered just messing enjoyably around, skiing, climbing, writing, spotting elks, painting pictures, making modest merry at the Springs. Their presence redeemed the old hotel for me, and as I eavesdropped upon their high-spirited gossip, their subterfuges for mollifying the immigration authorities, and their cheerful if impracticable ideas about how to raise the money for next month's rent, I thought them worthy successors to the statelier opportunists of old.

We went cross-country skiing in the morning — first thing in the bright, white, crunchy, wall-poster Banff morning. The temperature was minus thirty degrees Fahrenheit, and bundled to the eyebrows we set off along one of the snowy trails (an easy one, for my sake) that radiate around the resort. This suggested to me entering the pages of a nineteenth-century Rocky Mountain history book: a scene done in etching, or perhaps in lithograph, the trees extremely dark, the ground exceedingly white, and the well-wrapped figures of trappers, traders, or prospectors labouring on snowshoes through the forests of the West.

We ourselves were those toiling figures. We were as utterly alone, only a few miles from the Banff Springs Hotel, as if we really were looking for gold, or hunting for beavers, in the remotest mountain woodlands. We saw not another soul along that trail, heard not a sound but the cracking of ice sometimes, the distant rumble of an avalanche, and the confident swish of our skis, punctuated now and then by muffled oaths when I fell over.

When the brisk morning was done, I admitted to my companions not tiredness, of course, certainly not that, but perhaps a slight, perfectly pleasant, stiffening of the muscles. Easy to fix, said they. High above Banff are the hot springs that give the hotel its name, and stripping ourselves of our frozen accoutrements, into their sulphurous waters we shortly plunged. This was an eerie experience, I thought. The springs, fed into an open-air pool, emit dense clouds of steam, through which one dimly gropes and splashes, now and then discerning the hazy figures of fellow bathers, and occasionally, through a gap in the billowing vapour, catching a glimpse of the white mountain mass beyond.

The water is hot — as warm as a bathtub — but the air on a winter day is very, very cold. As one's body deliciously relaxes in the warm, one's hair becomes thickly and whitely frosted — one is hot and cold at the same time, fire and ice personified. There is something mythical or possibly volcanic to the sensation, and I felt myself brought prosaically down to earth when, pushing our way like performing dolphins through the swing-doors that separate the pool from the dressing room, we resumed our clammy clothing.

Mealtimes seem to mean nothing in Banff — any time is apparently eating time — so I'm not sure if it was a late luncheon or an early dinner that we now enjoyed at the Balkan. The retsina was indeed excellent, the atmosphere stimulating, the editor of the Banff *Crag and Canyon* stopped by for a drink, and an hour or two slipped by very easily before I telephoned the station to see how my train was coming along. Oh, running a bit behind schedule, they said in their Canadian way — nasty weather in the prairies, expect it to be three or four hours late in Banff.

That gave us time to go animal-watching. Every wild creature is protected within the Banff National Park, and so sure are the animals of their sanctuary that the life of the wilderness feels intimately close to the life of Banff itself, and you need not drive far from town to feel the presence of the beasts around you. For half an hour or so that evening, it is true, I saw nothing alive out there, only the limitless dark forest with its occasional snowy glades. But then I caught sight of something quite close to us in the shadows — a mule-deer, right there, just beside the road, its velvety Mickey Mouse ears scarcely bothering even to twitch as we passed by. And then, moving mysteriously across an icy meadow, a whole herd of elk — and a solitary coyote, meditatively pacing a frozen stream — and more elk — and another glimpse of deer — and eyes in the woods that I persuaded myself were cougar's, and footprints that I swear were grizzly bear's.

Primed with *moussaka* and retsina, without a gun between us, the Saab as snug and Swedish as could be — what *would* the old travelers have thought?

Almost before I knew it night had fallen. Keeping our eyes open for owls we scudded through the woodlands back to the railway station. My friend had to catch the end of a piano recital at the Fine Arts Centre, so there in the ice-cold darkness, my scarf around my face, feeling more like Anna Karenina than any peregrinating Edwardian duchess, I waited alone with my bags upon the platform, stamping my feet sometimes and blowing into my gloves, until Train 001 arrived like a giant out of the flatlands and took me off to the coast.

CHAPTER NINE

YELLOWKNIFE

IN *occupied territory*

I FLEW FROM HONG KONG
to the Northwest Territories to write this evocation of
Yellowknife, and when I saw the letters YK on a shopping
mall in town, instantly and foolishly I thought it must be
the property of Sir Y.K. Pao, one of the great magnates of
Hong Kong, who was universally known by his initials.

I was not so far off, either. Though the letters really
stood, of course, for Yellowknife itself, the shopping centre was indeed Hong Kong—owned, a fact that told me much
about the condition of the town. The very name of the place

*is synonymous for most of us with ice, cold, and infinite re-
moteness, and seen on the map Yellowknife is certainly well
on the way to the back of beyond. I soon discovered, however, that its real interest was not merely geographical —
nowadays it is far from inaccessible — but social, ethnic, economic, historical, and political, and it raised in
my mind all sorts of unexpected inquiries and allusions.*

*As a historian of the British Empire I was fascinated
by its colonial overtones. As an aficionado of Canada I
was entertained to see all the standard Canadian attitudes
transferred into this exotic setting. And as a romantic I
was moved to imagine, by the end of my time in YK, that
I had stumbled into one of the capitals of a federation yet
unborn.*

WHERE AM I? FROM MY
window I can see the downtown high-rise blocks, and watch
the birds strutting and squawking about the grass. I have a
luncheon date with the deputy minister of culture and communications; in the afternoon I'm on a radio chat-show. I
dine on a delicately smoked fish, rare steak with pâté, and
an honest Italian red, and after dinner I cross the road to
a book launch and signing party (canapés and some rather
good chocolate-covered cherries).

Where am I? I will give you some clues. The fish is arctic char, the meat is musk ox, the minister's cultural territories embrace a third of all Canada, the chat-show hostess
is a Dene, and the birds are those irrepressible rascals of

northern legend, those first cousins of the monkey-gods, the ravens.

I am in Yellowknife, "YK," capital city of the Northwest Territories, and if the opening of this essay seems to suggest a mixed bag of sensations, they are as nothing beside the complex and contradictory responses that beset me during my stay in this interesting but equivocal place. Only the ravens, I came to think, perpetually squabbling and thieving through the town, were altogether — well, I was going to say black and white, but you know what I mean.

I should lay my cards on the table. I spent only a week in Yellowknife. I was there in the fall, so that I experienced neither what I am assured are the glories of the all-but-nightless summer nor the gloomy fascination of the virtually dayless winter. Moreover I must confess that, a priori, Yellowknife is the kind of place turbocharged Ski-doos could not drag me to reside in.

The first impact of this town (population about 12,000) is, if not exactly a cliché yet, at least a truism. I had conditioned myself to expect, as most visitors do, a raw subarctic mining community — cold, racy, miscegenated, and probably drunk. I found, as I knew I would really, a complete small modern city, with malls, high-rise blocks, supermarkets, a posh hotel, book shops, computer stores, real-estate agents, brokers, an arts centre, a splendid museum, up-and-coming suburbs, a yacht club, and all the social paraphernalia of contemporary North American living, Kentucky Fried Chicken to (for the longitude is, after all, sixty-two degrees north) Daughters of the Midnight Sun.

140

This is because Yellowknife is above all an official town. These first appearances are like a hologram, as it were, of Ottawa, projected mundanely into these northern climes. After a day or two I seemed to feel, as in miasma around me, all the familiar matter of officialdom, all the preoccupations, the conventions, and the protocols, and walking along the city's perimeter one day I counted without surprise nineteen official flags flying from the rooftops of bureaucracy.

Presently it dawned upon me, too, that by today's standards sixty-two degrees is not very far north. There are settlements with supermarkets and air services far nearer the pole than this. You can drive from Edmonton to Yellowknife with perfect ease during all but a few weeks of the year, and tourism indeed is the city's second industry — after government, before gold-mining. The local publicity brochures list four hotels, two motels (I stayed very snugly at the Northern Lites), a YWCA, and Barb Bromley's Bed and Breakfast.

All in all, YK seemed to me at first rather an ordinary town; the frequent observation of its inhabitants, that it was a great place to bring up kids in, is what people say to me about rather ordinary small towns the world over.

But think of this: Yellowknife, capital of a region larger than India, is younger than I am — and good gracious, I am not all *that* old. Yellowknife was born in the 1930s, and some of the town's original settlers are still alive (though most of them now reside, I note, in warmer places far away).

For Yellowknife is an exciting rarity: a pioneer town of the air age. I have written about many frontier towns in my life, but never before I think about one that was established specifically by the agency of the airplane. The frontier is still

141

young here, the settlers are figures of the recent past, and once I had got used to the bureaucratic presence it was the legacy of the white prospectors and trappers that most immediately engaged me.

The new part of Yellowknife is built, to a grid, on higher ground above Great Slave Lake, and spreads away east and south in an uninspired expanse of suburban housing, trailer camps, and commercial this-and-that. On the peninsula that protrudes into the lake to the north, however, and on Latham Island at its tip (now un-islanded, actually, by a causeway) the first prospectors of Yellowknife unrolled their sleeping bags over fifty years ago. This is Old Town, and it remains very largely shackland still. The expensive new houses there, homes to Yellowknife's Yappies (young arctic upwardly mobile professionals), are still invested by a fine old muddle of makeshift.

There are fishing huts and warehouses and unexplained waterside constructions. There is a clump of gypsy-like shanties and outhouses, littered with Ski-doos, dog-huts, and pick-ups, inhabited largely by Alternative Persons and viewed with such pride by the Yellowknife tourist authorities that they offer a free walking guide to its dilapidations. There is a houseboat community off shore, and the original Wild Cat Café, Yellowknife's first eating place, and at the pier below Ragged Ass Street (a name Yellowknifers are quite touchingly proud of) fishermen bring in their catches from the cold, cold depths of the lake. The headquarters of Arctic Divers Ltd. is here, and so is the Hunters and Trappers Association; parked about the place you may see a pick-up announcing itself the property of Richard Beck, World Champion Dog Musher.

In the middle of Old Town protrudes a lump of the Precambrian shield, known simply as The Rock, upon whose slopes half a century ago the founding settlers pitched their tents and erected their huts in such profligacy, we are told, that one man's privy often blocked another man's front door. If the loveless concrete blocks of government are the most prominent symbols of contemporary Yellowknife, this rock is properly emblematic of the town's origins, and on the top of it they have erected a monument to the true begetters of the city, the bush pilots.

From up there the neat style of Yellowknife shows, especially when a bitter wind blows out of the north, making your eyes water and your ears tingle. Then the little city still looks dauntingly alone. Even the high-rise blocks look brave, against the interminable landscape of rock, frost, and stunted tree; even the four-star Explorer Hotel looks uncomfortably aware that the next comparable hostelry is 800 miles away. The jumble of Old Town seems insecurely deposited beside the formidable lake, with its lonely islands here and there and its inlets rimmmed with icy marsh; the chimneys of the town's two gold mines, one to the west, one to the east, puff their smoke into an unforgiving sky.

And everywhere there seem to be airplanes. The bush pilots memorialized on The Rock are flying still, and without them even now Yellowknife, capital of a third of Canada, would be impotent.

Looking from my window one evening I saw a single steadily burning light in the dusk sky. It seemed to be motionless — Jupiter somehow magnified in the subarctic air, I thought, or perhaps a UFO? Silently it hung there against the darkening sky, and only very slowly, majestically indeed, did it resolve itself into the form of a single small float-plane, bearing down on Yellowknife out of the north. Its light seemed so defiantly bright, the aircraft itself was so small, that when at last it landed with plumes of spray on the surface of the lake, I thought it a truly heroic image of Canada's northern adventure.

Until the road from Edmonton was completed, the only surface communication with Yellowknife from the south (canoe, sledge, or snowshoe apart) was by tractor-drawn trains of wagons which crunched their way brutally up here through the woodlands. Even now, in most parts of this city's hinterland, the million square miles over which it claims authority, one can travel only by air. An election was happening while I was in town, and nothing brought home this trackless state of things more tellingly than the spectacle of the candidates flying off, day after day, before dawn very often, to their remote and roadless hustings.

No wonder Yellowknife worships the airplane — the very first announcement of the city's presence, on its southern outskirts, is the lumpish Bristol Freighter, mounted on a plinth, which was the first wheeled aircraft ever to land at the North Pole. A spectacular showpiece of the Prince of Wales Northern Heritage Museum is a reconstructed de Havilland biplane, and indeed a marvellous variety of aircraft makes the whole town feel a repository of aviation history — the Boeing 737s and venerable Lockheed Electra turboprops with which Northwest Territorial Airways maintains its services, the DC3s that frequently come and go, the inescapable float-planes or the miscellaneously dismembered machines, reduced to their constituent floats, wings, and fuselages, which are left lying casually here and there about town.

All this, I thought, gave Yellowknife an imperial feeling. Although as a matter of fact this was never a great fur-trading centre, it seemed to me to stand directly in the line of the Hudson's Bay Company's forts and outposts, just as those planes were true successors to the canoes and dog teams of the explorers. Even in the prosaic centre of the new town there are echoes of the frontier. The jam-packed Bay is still very like a trading post. Miners, Indians, Métis, and Inuit eat their victuals in an authentic fug of warmth and chat in the Miner's Mess café at the Yellowknife Inn, and the frail and off-key voice of a girl singer in a tavern, sounding so innocent and courageous through the smoke, poignantly suggested to me the mores of gold rush and bawdyhouse.

But actually, if Yellowknife's original dominion was a dominion of the rough, the tough, and the nonconformist, since 1967, when the administrative centre of the NWT was moved here from Ottawa, it has been essentially a dominion of civil servants. Half the people of Yellowknife work for the government, and by and large they do not seem cast in the bush pilot, prospector, whorehouse mould. They have brought with them all the values of the Canadian south. They are extremely polite, very decent people I would judge, bourgeois, pretty dull of conversation. To see their children learning to skate at the rink is to see the best of them: the children so trimly helmeted and polychromatically padded, tumbling and skidding so adorably about the ice, the parents so touchingly proud and affectionate — "It's a great place," as they one and all assure me, "to bring up kids." To hear them addressing a public meeting is to experience them at their most depressing: oh, the long, slow, tuneless, humourless, saltless monotony of Canadian orthodoxy!

The offices of government are strewn through the town. Its manners and judgments are ubiquitous. Its courts of law, tabbed, gowned, and crested, might have been transported here *in toto* from southern Ontario. Its Mounties live next door to city hall, and just along the road, in a blue-painted complex of what looks like prefabricated laboratories, or perhaps discarded ships' containers, a brigadier general presides over Canada's Northern Region defence command. Calling in at the Explorer Hotel one day I found it taken over by swarms of officers from the National Defence College at Kingston, Ontario — looking, with their cloth caps, hacking jackets, and clipped moustaches, astonishingly like British Army officers of my youth.

Central to the official presence is the Council of the Northwest Territories, whose chamber is very properly attached to the back of the Yellowknife Inn. A visit to this legislature is one of the odder experiences of contemporary travel. Its members sit in two half-moon rows of seats, presided over by a Speaker, in an ambience blending North with South, Wild with Settled, Yellowknife with Ottawa, or perhaps Westminster with Arctic. The protocol is formal, the oratory is deadening, there are clerks and pages and a bemedalled ex-serviceman to carry the mace.

On the other hand the room is dominated neither by mace nor by Speaker but by the skin of a large polar bear whose head, still equipped with teeth and powerful jaws, glares

fiercely towards the public gallery. Pelts and artefacts of
the northlands decorate the walls, while embroidered seals,
bears, caribou, and other local fauna embellish the liv-
eries of the pages — who are, by the way, what with an
unremitting flow of notes between the various delegates,
and an apparently inflexible rule that they must bow to the
Speaker's chair every single time they pass it, kept as twitchy
as so many jack-in-the-boxes.

Actually one of these well-exercised junior functionaries
all but monopolized my attention during my visit to the
legislature of the Northwest Territories. She was about fifteen
years old, I would guess, indeterminately Caucasian, Indian,
Inuit, or Métis, and tremendous fun. Busy as she was taking
those perpetual missives from one member to another, and
incessantly bobbing to the chair, she managed to elevate
the whole session to a jollier and more sensible level. She
laughed to herself and to others, she did her bows with a
wonderfully comic jerkiness, she stuck her tongue out at
her colleagues, she yawned, she hitched her tights up, she
cheerfully swung her legs when she was sitting down, and
walked in a delightfully insouciant way when she was on her
feet. I loved this irrepressible child of the north; the legislators droned on as legislators will, but she brought a breath of
the woods inside.

Pottering around the more ramshackle end of Latham Island,
beyond the trendy part, I spotted a notice pinned to the
door of a hut. It said that Fur Payments Were Awaiting Peter
Drygeese and George Doctor, and so I realized that I was in an
enclave of the Dene, who are the original inhabitants of this

land, and whose settlements are scattered over thousands of square miles of the Northwest Territories.

The hut, it turned out, was the office of the Rainbow Band of the Dogrib. Their huts along the shoreline there are painted in now-faded primary colours, hence the name of the band — not in pursuance of any ancestral memory but because they were municipally tarted up for a visit years ago by the queen. Some of the huts have new bathroom annexes, recently supplied by the city at a cost greater, I was told, than the value of the houses themselves; but in general Rainbow Valley looks, I have to say, extremely hangdog.

A bit hangdog, too, look the Dene themselves, who together with Inuit, Métis, a few highly successful Chinese, and a handful of blacks, Japanese, and Vietnamese, give Yellowknife its ethnic tang. Dressed in a mixture of European and Indian clothes that I find difficult to identify, let alone describe, being more like the savouring of a soup than the soup itself — dressed, one might say, sort of Indianified — all too often the men seem to be swaying drunkenly at street corners, while the women wander apparently purposelessly through the Hudson's Bay store, or sit transfixed before "Days of Our Lives" at eleven in the morning. They appeared to have all the characteristics of a broken people, demoralized by history, and for my first few days the spectacle much depressed me.

But then I met a celebrated champion of the Dene, the Oblate Father René Fumoleau, who has lived among them for thirty-five years. We lunched together one day at the Great Gold City Emporium (I had fettucine with a glass of hot buttered rum, he had Caesar salad and beer), and he quite cheered me up about them. Far from being broken, he assured me, they were unbreakable. Certainly they had been debilitated by all the white man's familiar evils, alcohol to tuberculosis to drugs to crass materialism, but they themselves, and Father Fumoleau with them, were confident that they would survive as a people and as a culture.

After that I looked at the Dene in a different way, and sure enough came to perceive, I think, that their morosely passive air did not necessarily mean an acceptance of defeat. Some of them were certainly drunk, but others were vigorously sober at the Tree of Peace social centre. Some might look aimless, but some at least were purposeful at the Native Women's Association of the NWT. I like to think that after the fettucine, or perhaps it was the rum, I really did detect in them a dogged strength which may well outlive, as the priest believes, anything that southern society can throw at them.

The Dene Nation has its headquarters in Yellowknife, the focus of all its settlements and its several languages. Its current president lives at Dettah, a Dene village a few miles around the lake from Yellowknife, to which I paid a hopeful pilgrimage one bright and gusty Sunday morning. I was not instantly encouraged. A cluster of battered-looking wooden buildings by the lake, it was rather like a run-down fishing village somewhere in the Maritimes, I thought, with its beached boats, its piles of crates, its jetty, its lines of flapping washing, and its network of overhead telegraph wires, clustered windswept around a little white Catholic church.

But Mass was in progress when I arrived and, peering through a small unpainted segment of the church's interior door, I saw as a cameo the resident populace almost entire. It looked weather-beaten, reverent, earnest, attentive, and infinitely more dignified than it ever was hanging around the Yellowknife Inn. Two Catholic priests were in attendance, in full vestments, and through the door there came, sung in a dreary but invincible way that I now recognized as particularly Dene, a Gregorian chant with words that I took to be (in these post–Vatican II years) Dogrib.

Even Rainbow Valley came to seem, when I went back there, less depressing than I had first thought. It is true that some of its inhabitants live lives of sad indigence, but on the lake-edge the sled dogs of the band, chained to their home-made kennels, look wonderfully cocky, while out on the ice young Dogribs play a virile and sometimes hilarious hockey.

Nevertheless the longer I stayed in Yellowknife — the longer I stayed! a week in all! — the more it seemed to me like a town in an occupied territory, the Dene and Métis its subject peoples, the whites its overlords.

I am assured that the original pioneers, the prospectors, the bush pilots, the white trappers and traders, got on well enough with the natives. They pursued some of the same trades, if they hardly honoured the same spirits, and they frequently interbred. It was the arrival of government in 1967, together with the intrusions of corporate business into the Arctic regions, that gave Yellowknife its particular connotations of colonialism. After a time society here began to remind me uncannily of life at home in my own North Wales, where for more than 700 years the English have been occupying the territory of the racially, culturally, linguistically, historically, and perhaps spiritually different Welsh.

As I understand it, it is not that the southerners in Yellowknife — the whites, for want of a better generalization — are harsh or even overbearing towards the Indians. Nobody complained to me of racism, in any malicious personal sense. Nor are they politically despotic — of course they aren't. Dene and Métis not only provide half the members of the Territorial Council but occupy several government ministries too, while the proceedings are simultaneously translated into Chipewyan, South Slavey, North Slavey, Inuktitut, and Dogrib. Most whites I asked thought the recent well-publicized land deal between the federal government and the Dene-Métis leadership, which awards the natives title to vast tracts of territory, to be a fair and honest settlement of old grievances.

Yet to more sophisticated Dene the agreement is a betrayal of their most profound values — through all their history they have never aspired to be owners of the land, only its protectors and its subjects. Straightforward well-meaning Canadians from the south, I can well see, find such concepts hard to grasp, and I dare say most white Yellowknifers don't try too hard. Shop assistants, waitresses, and garage hands seem astonishingly ignorant about the very lie of the land, let alone the aspirations of its indigenes, while the miscellaneously bookish people I met over the chocolate cherries at that book launch appeared to know rather less about the geography of the Northwest Territories than I had, during the past twenty-four hours, picked up myself. I met nobody who expressed any ill will towards the natives, but few who could enlighten me about their culture — most of Yellowknife's whites, after all, spend only a couple of years here before returning to the south, and half the ones I encountered seemed to have arrived last Saturday week.

I write out of pure ignorance myself, of course, or at best out of hearsay and intuition, but I can report as facts many of the symptoms of contemporary colonialism that I recognize in Yellowknife precisely as I do at home. All the embarrassments and inhibitions of ethnic imposition are here to be observed: the familiar clashes between sympathy and ir- ritation, the tightrope passage between the friendly and the condescending, the sudden flares of underdog arrogance, the occasional bouts of paternalist despair, the expressions of resolute enjoyment and concern on the faces of liberals at drum chantings, the tortured sensitivities of address — I never could bring myself to ask anyone if he was an aboriginal, though I am told the word is perfectly acceptable, and was thus reduced to the prissy interrogation: "Excuse me, but may I ask — are you a *native person*?"

Then there is the whole vexed business of place names, familiar to any of us who have lived through the decline of the imperial idea. The fortnightly *Native Press*, I see, already calls Yellowknife Somba K'é, and one wonders how long it will be before Fort Wrigley permanently reverts to Tthedzéh Kóé or the poor old Mackenzie River becomes once more simply the Dehcho. And snarled up within it all — colonialists are always snarled up in one degree or another — the resident whites self- consciously assert identities of their own, so that shopkeepers are constrained to describe their establishments as Owned and

152

Operated by Northerners, and elderly ex-hippies are at pains to look Indianified themselves.

On the whole I believe Father Fumoleau when he promises me that the Dene and the Métis will still be here, still recognizably themselves, when many another generation of Ottawa administrators has come and gone from Yellowknife, and that perhaps one day they really will again rule their own destinies in their own way. Just for the moment, all the same, there is no denying that ethnically YK is all a bit of a mess.

I will tell you my own romantic and far-fetched recipe for the future of Yellowknife. I thought of it while looking at a geographical hemisphere in the Northern Heritage Museum — which really is, by the way, one of the very best such museums I have ever visited. This device displays the entire northlands of the world, set in a swath around the pole — all the lands of the Inuit, the Lapps, the Siberian nomads, the Dene themselves. In Yellowknife they are very fond of talking about The North, meaning in general any part of Canada north of the sixtieth parallel; but looking at this map I realized that there is a true northern unity extending far beyond Canada's own frontiers, and linked not only by climate and longitude but actually by race.

This made me see the town in a different light again. When I next looked from my windows upon that stupendous wilderness, hazed in the morning by steam rising Arthurianly from the surface of the lake, radiant in the evening with the dim, pale glow of the Arctic sun — now in my romantic way I fancied the little city of Somba K'é truly returned to its sovereign origins, liberated from all interferences and embarrassments, as one of the capitals of a circumpolar federation, a federation of the top of the world. Its peoples would be bound by a common spirituality, and its envoys would assemble from their fishing settlements, their trappers' hamlets, their ice-camps and mining towns around the perimeter of the Arctic, at their symbolic apex, the North Pole itself. Why not? The bush pilots could find it.

CHAPTER TEN

VANCOUVER

Too *nice for words?*

I DON'T KNOW WHY, BUT *this essay was not universally popular in Vancouver when it was first published in 1988. It was meant to be admiring on the whole, without being gushing, but from the point of view of the indigenes it evidently admired the wrong things. Also it concentrated upon the varying* niceness *of Vancouver, which is a quality the citizens, it seems, do not want to be associated with one way or the other.*

I had visited the city several times before, and have been often since, and though it has been greatly changed in re-

*cent years (especially by the influx of Hong Kong Chinese)
I have so far seen no reason to alter my views. Vancouver
is one of those cities, like San Francisco, which are the victims of their glorious settings. One expects too much of
them. As Californians like to say, there is less to them than
meets the eye. Vancouver looks the sort of town nearly
everyone would like to live in, and I imagine that residence
there can indeed be very agreeable. I write, though, as an
outsider, an itinerant, and with the best will in the world
I cannot resolve my equivocal feelings about the place.*

*I thought it an encouraging sign, all the same, and a
healthy corrective to the essay itself, that the reactions this
piece sparked among Vancouver's citizens were so often
not nice at all.*

I KNEW VANCOUVER AL-
ready, so even before I started on the long journey west from
New York City I had devised an opening for this essay. I was
going to begin with a defence of the adjective "nice."

Pedants maintain that it can be synonymous only with "precise," or perhaps "delicate," as in a delicate balance, but you
and I know of course that it is a synonym too for Canada,
and in particular for that quintessence of Canadianness in its
most amiable kind, the city of Vancouver — whose reputation is nothing if not tolerant, whose appearance is always
seemly, whose temper is famously kind, and whose stance
between the mountains and the sea is a model of municipal
etiquette.

But when I reached the city this time the analogy seemed less absolute than I had thought before. 1987's Vancouver seemed no longer pure nice, plain nice, but variously neo-nice, semi-nice, post-nice, over-nice, or even a little anti-nice. It seemed to be toying with its own character, not sure whether to modify it or make the most of it — as people sometimes do too, when they grow tired of their own personalities.

I scrapped my projected paragraph and, opening my typewriter upon a bench in Stanley Park, began again.

It never rains in Vancouver — I have been here six times now, so I know this for a fact. Also nobody has to work, nobody is sick, and you can leave your front door unlocked when you go away. Basking in perpetual sunshine, with no commitments, no financial worries, no pressure of competition, and blissfully happy marriages one and all, Vancouver is a city whose inhabitants are people of the Blessed Isles, spared all wars and natural calamities, spared even the miseries of urban decline, political corruption, rush-hour hassle, or juvenile delinquency.

If you doubt all this, look about you now, upon the seashore walk around the lovely park, and observe those inhabitants for yourself. They move unreally through an almost unreal environment, where never a dog defecates or a garbage can spills, and where even the big black crows refresh themselves decorously at drinking fountains. How clean they look, how sensible, how content! Barefoot children in long dresses build sand castles on the glistening flats, the sailboats shifting blue and white behind them as in a Boudin painting. Preternaturally slim elderly ladies lie behind driftwood windbreaks, wearing bikinis with perfect propriety and reading romantic fiction. Joggers bound by in supple rhythm. Scrubbed, polite, law-abiding youths swoop athletically about on bicycles. And what have those young people written in such large letters in the sand? Why, HAVE A NICE DAY of course — what else?

But one need not parody, or even exaggerate, the pleasantness of Vancouver. This is, one might say, the last resort of pleasantness, and especially, I think, pleasantness of a middle-class, middle-income, middle-aged Englishy kind. A metropolis of 1.3 million people, of innumerable nationalities, it still has the public manners of an English country town half a century ago. It seldom raises its voice. It would not dream of jumping a light. During ten days in Vancouver I never heard a car horn tooted.

Physically it is just as considerate, too. The promontory which stands at the heart of it is everyone's downtown ideal: residential beside commercial, working port beside tourist attraction, the whole elegantly framed by a backdrop of sea and snow-topped mountain range. Its high-rise buildings (nothing so aggressive as a real skyscraper) are generally discreet, its shops and restaurants are fun. It enjoys a proper contemporary mix of Chinese, Japanese, and miscellaneously ethnic neighbourhoods, and is modestly sprinkled, as by enlightened planners of the 1950s, with manifestations of harmless sleaze (Female Bar Wrestling at Doc's, or Miss Nude Orient '87, Direct from Hong Kong).

And all around this exquisitely balanced core, through the inevitable miles of suburbs, there is almost nothing ugly —

ordinary of course, monotonous sometimes, but seldom offensive. Refreshing parks abound and glorious excursions beckon: along spectacular fjords in steam trains, among forested islands by boat, to waterside cafés for oysters and chips, up unfrequented creeks to watch the grebes bobbing in the tidewater, or spot the spectral blue herons motionless on the flats.

Except for its trees and mountains, the scene has little in common with the rest of Canada. Its light is the pale, moist Pacific light that illuminates San Francisco too, and its colours are fresh buoyant colours, yellows, and pinks, and easy greys, such as restaurateurs all down this coast use when they want to emphasize the abalonic or salmonian nature of their cuisine. Vancouver is not a bronzed city, for all the exposure of those women on the beach; its complexions are sensitive, like its tastes, and its gardens are very, very green.

Dear me, how well everything works. After the incompetent decay of the New York telephone system, Vancouver's seems a very paragon of courteous modernity. Quiet, frequent, meticulously driven are the buses. Sleek and smooth is the SkyTrain, sliding on its elevated tracks above the suburbs. Majestically accelerates the catamaran SeaBus across the Burrard Inlet. There are taxis especially humped to accommodate wheelchairs in Vancouver, and talking elevators for the blind, and the aerial tramway that runs up to the summit of Grouse Mountain every day is operated by brisk, well-exercised girls of unimaginable helpfulness.

But then helpfulness, thoughtfulness, caringness if you can stomach the word, are standard attributes of Vancouver. This city pullulates with good intentions — saving Indian heritages, preventing the destruction of forests, avoiding wars, raising money for medical research, feeding the Third World — causes social, religious, political, ecological, environmental, or just generically moral. I doubt if there is another city in the world more preoccupied with goodness, and it is only natural that Vancouver's most popular citizen, at the time of my most recent visit, should be Rick Hansen, who propelled his wheelchair around the entire world on behalf of the disabled, and who is to the people of Vancouver what Rambo might be, perhaps, to the people of Detroit.

I went one day to the Law Courts, and thought I had never visited a building so comfortingly expressive of *concern*. If anything could represent in masonry the text This Is Going To Hurt Me More Than It Hurts You, or I'm Not Angry With You, Only Disappointed, this building does it. Designed by Vancouver's most celebrated architect, Arthur Erickson, structurally it might double as the Hanging Gardens of Babylon, or as the foyer of a Hyatt hotel, but metaphysically it is like the consulting room of some cosmic psychiatrist. Soft, how soft are its seats, gentle, how gentle its lights, soothingly silent is its air conditioning, unalarming its décor, and within it the majesty of the British Columbian version of Canadian law is exerted, it seems to me, with a lack of all rancour or reproach.

It is Vancouver's virtues crystallized. In what other courthouse on earth would one hear a lawyer say, as I heard it said in this most reassuring hall of justice, "You're faced, ladies and gentlemen of the jury, with two very, very nice people, the plaintiff, and the defendant. . . ."

Does it sound a bit boring? Well, yes, perhaps it is a bit. Vancouver's merits are not terribly exciting, and they are masked anyway in an all-too-becoming reserve. Its two news-papers, both owned by the same chain, must surely rank high among the dullest journals in the English language. Nobody whistles in its streets. It swarms with British immigrants who are neither quite one thing nor altogether the other, and with British expatriates of the sort who like to call themselves — ugh! — Brits.

All Canada is reserved, undemonstrative, unassuming. I put it down variously to the size of the country, the generally daunting climate, the lingering influence of those Brits and their debilitating traditions, and the presence of the marvellous, mighty, and terrible neighbour to the south. In Vancouver, however, decorum assumes a new dimension, and gives the whole city (to a stranger's sensibility, anyway) a peculiarly tentative air.

Consider the Smile Test. This is the system I employ to gauge the responsiveness of cities everywhere, and it entails smiling relentlessly at everyone I meet walking along the street — an unnerving experience, I realize, for victims of the experiment, but an invaluable tool of investigative travel journalism. Vancouver rates very low in the Smile Test: not, heaven knows, because it is an unfriendly or disagreeable city but because it seems profoundly inhibited by shyness or self-doubt.

Pay attention now, as we put the system into action along Robson Street, the jauntiest and raciest of Vancouver's downtown boulevards. Many of our subjects disqualify

161

themselves from the start, so obdurately do they decline eye contact. Others are so shaken that they have no time to register a response before we have passed by. A majority look back with only a blank but generally *amenable* expression, as though they would readily return a smile if they could be sure it was required of them, and were quite certain that the smile was for them and not somebody else. A few can just summon up the nerve to offer a timid upturn at the corners of the mouth, but if anybody smiles back instantly, instinctively, joyously, you can assume it's a visiting American, an Albertan, or an immigrant not yet indoctrinated.

The buildings conform. Vancouver enjoys one of the most splendid of all city settings — better than San Francisco's, because of the greenness, better than Sydney's, because of the mountains all around, rivalled perhaps only by Rio and Hong Kong. It is almost as though the surroundings have been artificially landscaped, on the most colossal scale, and this necessarily gives the city an exhibition flavour, as if consciously on display.

Even to the best of Vancouver architecture — even to Simon Fraser University among its greeneries, or the marvellous UBC Museum of Anthropology with its Indian-y crossbeams — there seems to me a lack of spontaneity. This city is all malls, all pavilions, all exhibition halls, all progressively laid-out markets. Sustained as it is by the Vancouver genius for keeping everything in a condition of pristine impeccability, it implants in my mind an impression of permanent newness, un-ageable, un-soilable, un-crackable, lichen-less, and creeper-free unless otherwise architecturally stipulated.

It *is* new, of course. There is hardly a building in the entire city more than a century old, but so perfectly is everything cherished and maintained that even the oldest feels far younger still. This gives the city a sense of flat time-lessness that I find rather dispiriting, but which adequately reflects, I suppose, the flatness of the city's style.

Consider Gastown, for instance, which is the oldest part of Vancouver and is named for Gassy Jack Deighton, a talkative early publican of the town. Even in my own memory Gastown used to be run-down enough for the most perversely nostalgic tastes, but it has been enthusiastically restored, and is now so assiduously paved and picturesque, so pretty with kiosks and ornamental lamp standards, so whimsically crowned by its Steam Clock, whose vapours drift evocatively among the sidewalk trees, that nobody would suppose it for a moment to be anything but contemporary pastiche.

It is a queer characteristic, this truncating or levelling of time. It makes Vancouver feel simultaneously young and geriatric, and perhaps has something to do with the spring-like, Elysian, lotus-and-asphodel quality of the place. Some-times from my hotel window I used to see a replica stern-wheeler, the *Constitution*, churning its way upon a tourist circuit past the massed woodlands of Stanley Park, beneath the arch of the Lions Gate Bridge (known also, and more lyrically I think, as the First Narrows Bridge), and out to the open sea.

It was always a fine sight, that little white ship, froth at the stern, chugging out beneath the mountains — so small, brave, and perky against the immensity of the scene. To my surprise, though, I was never *moved* by it. It seemed absolutely part

of the place and the time. It evoked no sense of high anachronism, suggested no romance. It was all clean, all new, all
spick-and-span, all ageless. If you smiled at the *Constitution*,
I bet you anything it would not smile back.

Halfway through my visit, something cracked in me.

Walking along a pleasant wooded track on Grouse
Mountain, where those well-exercised girl attendants had
deposited me for an hour of recreation, I was attacked by a
mad ptarmigan. It lay in wait for me beside the path and, as
all unsuspecting I rambled by, it hurled itself upon my ankles,
uttering sinister gurgles and prancing around me in so crazed
a way that I was obliged to beat it off with my handbag.

This grotesque scene, high up there above the city, had for
me an allegorical or mythical meaning, for I knew exactly
how that bird felt. I too had come to think, during my stay
in Vancouver, that I would like to wring the necks of the
more impassive passersby, dance dementedly around them,
or make peculiar noises. I too found myself exasperated by the
self-control, the moderation, the logic of everything, and was
tempted towards antisocial activities, like scrawling graffiti
on those courthouse walls, or driving my rented car at nine-
ty around Stanley Park Drive, blowing the horn and allowing
hard rock to blare through my open windows.

After five days, you see, I was pining for imperfection or
excess. I pined for the dingy, the neglected, and the disregarded old, for a scowl now and then, for swagger, for
flash, for a snatch of Brooklyn raucous, Strine conceit, Scouse
irreverence. I pined for blacks, punks, French Canadians,
yes, Torontonians. I would not go so far as to say I pined

for AT&T, but I did occasionally wish those girls would press the wrong button on the Grouse Mountain tramway, or that the SeaBus would break down in mid-crossing and be carried floundering ludicrously out to sea.

The ptarmigan, recognizing perhaps that we had something in common after all, begrudgingly broke off the engagement after a few moments, and retreated skulking into the woods.

When I told Vancouver people about my preposterous encounter with the bird, they were not at all surprised or entertained. "You should go to Lighthouse Park," they said, "you often see bald eagles there," or, "Did you know they're putting a loon on one side of the dollar coin?" At first I thought this was just another symptom of their indigenous tact, but later I began to think they themselves might have a sneaking empathy for the ptarmigan's paranoia.

For by no means all Vancouverites are content with their civic flavour. Only one in thirty-six of them, I am authoritatively assured (by a woman I met at Safeway), was actually born in this city, but perhaps they are vicariously nostalgic for Vancouver's rip-roar days of old, days of Gassy Jack and Silly Billy Frost, days when the smell of dogfish oil hung on the morning air, when you paid for your pre-breakfast whisky with gold dust on the counter, and at the House of the Nations, so it was said in 1919, a man could "get everything from a chocolate coloured damsel to a Swedish girl." "Feral" is an adjective that recurred in conversation, and possibly Vancouverites hunger for some revived ferality in themselves.

Many of them were anxious to show me something ruffianly. Everyone, even the most genteel, urged me to take a walk along East Hastings Street, where a few half-heartedly inebriated Indians, and a scattering of panhandlers and unobtrusive layabouts, still offer a wan impersonation of Skid Row. Everyone told me to eat at The Only Cafe, a counter joint of legendary rough-and-readiness — "They don't even have a washroom!" "The Wild West!" exclaimed my young taxi driver one evening, pointing out to me with satisfaction an old man with one trouser leg rolled up dancing to a sidewalk guitar.

But they need not have pressed their case, for I knew well enough, really, that Vancouver was not just a town of tame gentility. Claims or complaints reached me every day of political mayhem, financial malpractice, academic intrigue, and racial bigotry. I heard of inter-Sikh hostilities, of South American drug smugglings, of currency racketeers and flamboyantly shady entrepreneurs. If I was told once I was told a dozen times about the local luminary accused of profiting from pornography, and the captain of industry with a taste for flagellatory teenage prostitutes. . . .

Besides, I had only to look around me, almost anywhere, to know that this is a city built not upon respectable appearances, but upon brawn. The yellow mounds of sulphur on the shores of Burrard Inlet — the mist of grain around the north shore elevators — the long lines of wagons rolling always along the bayshore railway tracks — the huge log jams of the Fraser River, the tugs with their barges, the hefty foreign freighters swinging with the tide — the constant traffic of the sea planes, splashing their rumps in the water as they lurch to a landing — the thicketed masts of the fishing fleets jam-packed at their Steveston quays — the bright-lit floating fuel-stations of Coal Harbour, in sleepless echelon through the night — the ferries perpetually on the move, the helicopters whirring across the water, the futuristic liners moored below the billowing white tent-shapes of Canada Place — all these are inescapable reminders that Vancouver is really a place of virile meaning.

Above all perhaps the sea planes, for though they are part of Vancouver's time warp, especially the ones with bulbous radial engines like aircraft of the 1930s, still they tell us how close this city is to wild and inaccessible places. Only a few miles outside its limits, all suggestion of civility evaporates. Go one way and you are in the fierce mountain country, where the peaks called The Lions peer with a distinct malevolence, I always think, over the shoulders of the foothills to the city below. Go another and you are in the dank marshlands that fringe the Fraser estuary, soggy salt-flat country where cattle graze among the sedge, seabirds whirl, and grey radar installations stand hunched eerily in the waste.

And of course this is Indian country. There are Coast Salish reserves near the centre of the city, bringing a welcome touch of the gypsy to its tidiness. I called one afternoon at the house of one of Vancouver's best-known and best-paid artists, a delectable immaculate affair of mellow woods and split levels which might have been in any particularly expensive quarter of any well-heeled city of the Western world. Literally just around the corner, just a block away, I found a reserve of the Musqueam band, who have been in these parts since the start of time, whose language was born of the north wind, whose ancestral spirits were the spirits of the beginning of things, and whose backyards are triumphantly elemental with wheel-less limousines, unpainted boats on chocks of bricks, and flapping strings of washing.

The matter of the Indians runs deep in Vancouver, and does something to undermine the cool of the place. It is queer to remember, looking out upon this city's prospects, or for that matter coasting through the residential streets of the Musqueam band, that not so very long ago all this country was the domain of another culture altogether. One of Vancouver's most eminent citizens is the artist and carver Bill Reid, half-Haida himself and the Haida's grand protagonist, whose images of raven and owl, serpent and killer whale can hardly be escaped even by the hastiest visitor to the city.

I went to visit this old champion at his studio in Vancouver, and more than anything else the experience brought to life for me the immemorial human presence that preceded and underlies this particularly modern city. He showed me the great ocean-going canoe he had built for Expo 86, at present upside down in a shed but still magical with gleam and craftsmanship. With a few bold strokes he drew a whale for me. But I most enjoyed just watching him wandering around his workshop, where three young Haida apprentices were working upon totem poles (the totem pole market being bullish just now): a formidable stooped figure, rather pale, moving slowly here and there among the work tables, sometimes bending to check the elevation of a dogfish, sometimes picking up a knife to chip a raven beak or sharpen the teeth of a bear — carrying within himself, I thought, in this calm contemporary place, a power incongruously old, tragic, and elusive.

Underneath a road bridge, at the top of False Creek, is the small peninsula miscalled Granville Island, once the city's manufacturing vortex, now transformed into a mixed enclave of arts, tourism, commerce, and surviving industry, with an esteemed brewery, a popular food market, yacht basins, craft shops, boat repairers, cappuccino cafés, a school of art, a houseboat community, and Bill Reid's studio. It has been kept quite deliberately higgledy-piggledy, down to the disused railway tracks still running through it — "This realm," says a planner's memo in the information office, "must be Robust" — and it offers the visitor the rare Vancouver pleasure of socially acceptable jaywalking.

Vancouverites are proud of this delightful little retreat, and indeed sometimes talk of it as being the True Heart of Vancouver. This only confirms my suspicion that, like many another Canadian community, Vancouver is yearning for self-release. It is a city, one feels, that wants to be something else — like a chrysalis approaching metamorphosis. It surely cannot stay as it is forever, eternally young, eternally diffident, defying all the odds of urban development. Vancouver feels half-empty to me, though natives complain of its growing congestion, and half-fulfilled as well.

Sometimes I think the yearning, in its inchoate way, is just a yearning for mystery or surprise. The totem poles which stand here and there within the municipality, clumped so unexpectedly in Stanley Park, dreaming arcanely in the sun outside the Museum of Anthropology, are evidence of a past that is almost lost: but they also seem to represent a desire

— the very desire that I feel myself, among so much neatness and rational conduct, for that element of the transcendental, the immaterial, the instinctive, the unexplained, which comes from a sense of wider meanings and more universal standards.

More prosaically, I sense the city worrying its way towards a closer involvement with the world at large. Isolated here on its idyllic shore, thousands of miles from its own federal capital, a wilderness to the north of it, a foreign country to the south, Vancouver feels particularly alone. One of its dreams now is the dream of pan-Pacificism, based upon the theory that the Pacific Ocean is becoming the world's epicentre, and that the cities all around its rim are destined to form a great brotherhood of mutual prosperity.

According to this fantasy Vancouver would discover a new self in pan-Pacificism (a self, I suspect, not unlike that of Sydney, a city towards which Vancouverites seem to look with almost pathetic envy). It would become a teeming metropolis of banks, investment houses, and cosmopolitan speculators, electronically hyperactive twenty-four hours a day — all flickering computer screens, shirtsleeved money manipulators keyed in to Tokyo and Hong Kong, power breakfasts with Japanese brokers at the Vancouver Club.

And to a degree it is happening. The Asians are certainly coming, whether they be sushi masters or trade delegates; so rich is the town in Oriental faces that Vancouver's long-established Chinatown is hardly noticeable these days. Wide expanses of downtown belong to Hong Kong interests, the Bank of British Columbia is a subsidiary of the Hong Kong Bank, the Pan Pacific Hotel is Japanese-owned, and one is not at all surprised to find that the Gr. Sun Yat-Sen Classical Garden, said to be the finest outside China, has been financed by such scholarly philanthropists as British Columbia Telephones and the Canadian Imperial Bank of Commerce. (So pervasive are these developments actually that for some time I assumed the logo of the Royal Bank of Canada, which depicts a sort of squashed-up lion holding an orb, to be a Chinese ideogram.)

But it is hardly fulfilment yet, and Vancouver has scarcely been galvanized into greatness by the Pacific brotherhood. Unemployment is very high in this city, many a new office block looks for tenants, and, though a student acquaintance of mine observes bitterly that it's a great place to live in if you're rich (she isn't), still I notice that plenty of houses are for sale in the up-market, rock-garden, mullion-windowed suburbs. I am told in fact that much Japanese investment, and much Hong Kong funk money, prefers to leapfrog Vancouver and go direct to Toronto — you don't have to be on the ocean these days to qualify as a city of the Pacific Rim.

Anyway, however Asian it becomes, however pan-Pacific, Vancouver will doubtless always depend upon the old staples of its economy, upon the lumber industry, upon the port trade, upon tourism, upon canning and fishing and milling and refining. If I dare make a prophecy, as a matter of fact, I would myself hazard an unpopular guess that in fifty years' time Vancouver will be much as it is today, only less so.

Less pristine and meticulous, that is, for even Vancouver cannot permanently escape the urban rot. Less fresh-faced and imperturbable, as the ethnic balance shifts. Less reserved and unassertive, perhaps, as competition bites. Less orderly and uptight, as the legacy of the British wanes at last. Less restrained and considerate, as the free trade in violence and vulgarity inexorably proceeds.

Less beautiful? I think not — nothing can really spoil the natural glory of it. Less boring? Oh certainly, sure to be less boring.

If for nothing else, I have high hopes for improved performance in the Smile Test. It would be one in the eye for visiting know-alls if Vancouver's unexciting decency proved a match for the world's corrosion after all, and the characteristics I have been sneering at turned out to be this city's strengths. And perhaps they will. . . .

It happened that during my stay in town Rick Hansen returned home at the end of his wheelchair circumnavigation, and I went to the reception offered to him by the province and the city in British Columbia Place, "the world's largest air-supported domed stadium."

Some 50,000 citizens went too, but the occasion was not what I had expected, suggesting to me as it did a cross between a Hollywood game show, a revivalist meeting, and May Day in Bulgaria. There were twirling hordes of folk dancers, and armies of screaming children, and gigantically amplified rock songs, and a military band, and a show biz host, and Mr. Mulroney on an enormous video screen, and the premier's wife in a yellow headband, and thousands of tirelessly applauding senior citizens, and a film crew of course, and half the wheelchairs of the Western hemisphere, and Mr. Hansen himself doing a round of honour before ascending the ceremonial ramp to deafening adulation — "Rick, you're Fan-Tas-Tic!" — and a plethora of inspirational messages.

This was another Vancouver. It was entirely benevolent, as you would expect. Its cause was admirable, it goes without saying. Its fervours were harmless, like the fervours of royalism, say. Its hero behaved stylishly. But taken aback as I was by the frenzied hoopla of it all, I found myself viewing the festivities with a curmudgeonly eye. You could make this lot cheer anything, I heard myself grumbling. Why don't they go the whole hog, and lick the fellow's boots? Have they got a fixation about wheelchairs? Join the bandwagon, Mr. Mulroney. Smile this way please, Mrs. Vander Zalm!

It was sour grapes, of course, but you must make allowances. The energy of Canadian niceness, like the force of Canadian ennui, can be disconcerting to the foreigner.

This book is set in Garamond, a typeface designed in 1545 by Claude Garamont, a punch cutter in Paris. The face seen on these pages is the best of the modern revivals of this letterform, which gained popularity in the early seventeenth century. It is light in "colour," delicate in design, and yet smoothly legible. The roman has a certain "prickle" to the eye and the italic an erratic twist. It is one of the finest old styles ever cut.

Jacket and book design by Robert Priest
Illustrations by Barry Blitt